DISCOVERING THE ORIGINS OF MAN

DISCOVERING
THE ORIGINS
OF MAN

by Leslie Aiello

Published by

STONEHENGE

in association with

The American Museum of Natural History

The author

Dr. Leslie Aiello is a lecturer in Anthropology at University College, London. A graduate of the University of California, Los Angeles, she gained a PhD from the University of London for her research in the early evolution of human walking. Dr. Aiello has participated in excavations in Iran and is currently involved in the study of ape fossils in Kenya. She is on the council of the Primate Society of Great Britain.

The consultants

Dr. Bernard Campbell is Adjunct Professor of Anthropology at the University of California, Los Angeles. Educated at Cambridge University, he is the author of many articles and books. He has taught at Cambridge and Havard Universities as well as at the University of California, and carried out research in East Africa, South Africa and Iran. As a palaeoanthropologist, his central interest is the evolution of human behavior.

Dr Eric Delson is Professor of Anthropology at Lehman College and the Graduate Center, City University of New York, and Research Associate in Vertebrate Paleontology, the American Museum of Natural History. A graduate of Harvard College who received his PhD from Columbia University, he is the author or co-author of numerous articles and a book on the evolution of higher primates. His main current research project is the analysis of the fossil monkeys from Pliocene and Early Pleistocene hominid sites in Africa, with the eventual aim of refining the chronology of human evolution.

The American Museum of Natural History

Stonehenge Press wishes to extend particular thanks to Dr. Thomas D. Nicholson, Director of the Museum, and Mr. David D. Ryus, Vice President, for their counsel and assistance in creating this volume.

Stonehenge Press Inc.:
Publisher : John Canova
Editor : Ezra Bowen
Deputy Editor : Carolyn Tasker

Trewin Copplestone Books Ltd :
Editorial Consultant : James Clark
Managing Editor : Barbara Horn

Created, designed and produced by
Trewin Copplestone Books Ltd, London

© Trewin Copplestone Books Ltd, 1982

Library of Congress Card Number : 81-51993
Printed in U.S.A. by Rand McNally & Co.
First printing

ISBN 0-86706-006-9
ISBN 0-86706-058-1 (lib. bdg.)
ISBN 0-86706-027-1 (retail ed.)

Set in Monophoto Rockwell Light by
SX Composing Ltd, Rayleigh, Essex, England
Separation by Gilchrist Bros. Ltd, Leeds, England

Contents

The World of Human Origins

The search for the origins of man has all the makings of a great mystery story. There are clues – a bit of bone here, a few teeth there – and detectives in the guise of scientists from more than a dozen different disciplines, each keen to find another piece in the jigsaw puzzle that is man's ancestry.

Anthropologists are the key detectives in this fascinating search for human origins. These are the people who specialize in the study of mankind – that is, the way humans live now as well as the way their ancestors are thought to have lived in the past. Physical anthropologists focus on the comparative anatomy of present-day humans, as well as those whose bones and teeth have been preserved in the form of fossils, and the other primates considered to be man's closest relatives. The primates are those animals, including man, with relatively large brains, forward facing eyes and grasping hands.

Cultural or social anthropologists focus on the more speculative aspects of man's lifestyle – how communities were structured, for example, or whether man's ancestors hunted alone or with others.

Both types of anthropologists, however, pay special attention to the changes that have taken place, in both form and behavior, as man and the other living creatures have attempted to adapt to the world around them. This study of the changes, frequently referred to as evolution, requires some knowledge of anatomy (the study of bone and skeleton size and shape) and zoology (the study of animals, particularly the monkeys and apes).

Geologists, those who focus on the history of the earth as it is recorded in rock formations, are also pivotal characters in the search for human origins, for it is this discipline that provides dates for much of what the anthropologists recover.

Paleontologists (specialists in the study of fossil animals) and archaeologists who focus on cultural artifacts such as tools or shrines, also contribute facts and theories to anthropology.

A few individuals involved in this exciting search combine several specialities. These people, usually in charge of a particular fossil-bearing site, are called paleoanthropologists.

Since the early nineteenth century, the scientific detectives trying to solve the puzzle of man's origins have developed a vocabulary unique to their field. *Hominid* is the name given to the primate group that includes present-day man, earlier subspecies and such ancient and mysterious creatures as *Australopithecus* and *Ramapithecus*. In this specialized vocabulary, the words "human" and "modern man" take on very particular meanings. For anthropologists, *humans* are those people living today as well as those in the recent past who are anatomically identical to living man. *Modern* refers to the fossils considered more like present-day humans than other hominids.

Homo, the Latin word for man, is the name assigned to those fossils that appear to be more like modern man than like the older *Australopithecus* specimens. There are several types of *Homo*, chiefly *Homo habilis* (for handy man in recognition of his assumed ability to make and use stone tools), *Homo erectus* (so-named for his upright posture), and finally *Homo sapiens* (after the Latin word for wise).

Although *Homo sapiens* has been around for as much as 100,000 years – and possibly longer – scientists can not yet agree when this name should first be used.

Considering all the possible clues and the different paths the scientists have to follow, it is no wonder that the search for human origins is still an open case. New discoveries frequently blow apart carefully reasoned theories. One fossil date that does not mesh with the archaeological evidence can re-open a closed case. In all likelihood, the search for the origins of man will continue as long as there are people willing to hunt for that one key piece of evidence – be it bone or tooth or complete skeleton.

A Look at Mankind

The scientific name for the human species is *Homo sapiens*, which means "wise man" or "understanding man" in Latin. Man is different from any other form of life on earth in the extent of his ability to think, understand, change, use and control the world around him. This ability is called intelligence.

Physical anthropologists are the specialists who piece together scientific information to try to reconstruct how humans have adapted to the changing world throughout time. To understand the similarities and differences between man and the other modern animals most closely related to him, such as the apes, they study and compare the body form, behavior, and environment of humans and such animals. From fossils and other remains of ancient forms of life anthropologists can record the specific changes that have occured in evolution. From the rocks in which the fossils are found scientists can often determine what the earth was like when these fossilized animals were alive.

The first step in the study of human evolution is to recognize those features that distinguish man from other animals. Together with intelligence, these features form the basis of man's position in the animal world and hold the clues to human evolution.

Man is the only species that habitually stands and moves in an upright position. Human feet, knees, pelvis and the vertebrae of the spinal column are specially adapted to bipedalism (two-footed walking). Moving bipedally means the hands are free to make, use and carry the tools that are essential to man's way of life.

Another important distinction between man and other animals is the relative proportions of heads and faces. Humans have large brains, so that the part of the head that houses the brain is large by comparison with the face, jaws, and teeth, which in humans lie below the braincase or cranium, not in front of it as in other animals. Humans have larger brains in relation to their body size than most other animals. Although human intelligence can be generally related to the high ratio of brain size to body size, there are also important differences in the structure of the brain that are related to intelligent behavior and the ability to use language.

The shape, structure, and position of the teeth of an animal species, and the patterns of wear on them, provide information about that species' diet. A close look at modern man's teeth reveals several unique characteristics. The teeth in both jaws form a con-

The skulls of baboons (right) and gorillas (center) have much smaller braincases (craniums) and larger faces than that of a modern human being (far right). When the brain size is compared to the body weight of each creature the human has a brain two and a half to three times as large as the brain of the gorilla or the baboon. The gray areas show side views of the creatures' heads as they would appear in life.

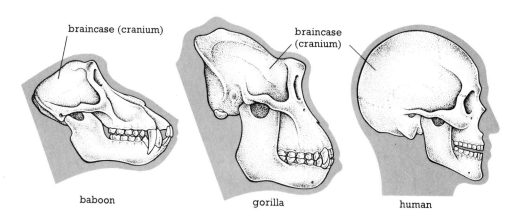

braincase (cranium)

braincase (cranium)

baboon

gorilla

human

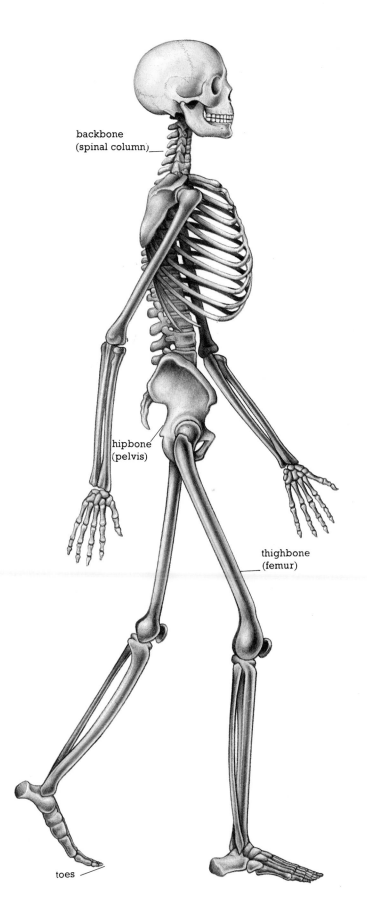

backbone
(spinal column)

hipbone
(pelvis)

thighbone
(femur)

toes

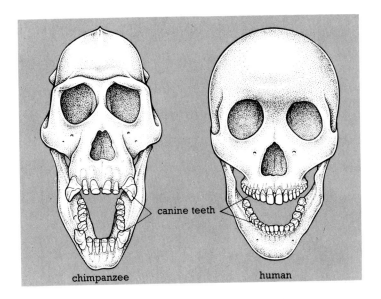

canine teeth

chimpanzee   human

This diagram shows the difference in the shape of the jaw and the size of the teeth in a chimpanzee (left) and a modern human being (right). As a chimpanzee eats, its large projecting canine teeth overlap each other, so the jaws cannot move sideways. In contrast human canine teeth do not overlap, so that when eating the jaws can move up and down or from side to side to grind as well as tear food.

tinuous curved line, with no projecting canine teeth at the front corners of the jaws. Human teeth are covered in thick enamel which makes them resistant to harsh foodstuffs. These features suggest that human ancestors had a different type of diet from most other primates (those animals, such as apes and monkeys, that are related to humans).

Man's abilities and body form today are the result of millions of years of gradual change and adaptation to the altering conditions of life. It is the study of these changes, where and why they happened, that forms the fascinating story of man's evolution.

This is how a modern human skeleton looks when it is in the walking position. Humans have shorter toe-bones, longer femurs and shorter, wider hipbones than a gorilla. These features enable humans to walk upright easily all the time, while gorillas only walk upright some of the time.

Man's Primate Relatives

In all the animal kingdom it is the great apes (the chimpanzee, gorilla, and orangutan) that are most similar to man in details of their bodies and skeletons. Scientists describe man and the great apes as primates, along with gibbons of Asia, and monkeys in Africa, Asia and Central and South America. There are also more primitive primates that have smaller brains, for example the lemurs on the island of Madagascar, the lorises of southeast Asia and the bush-babies of Africa.

All non-human primates have hands like humans'. The thumbs are opposable, that is, they are separated from the fingers and can move independently from them, giving all primates the ability to reach out and grasp objects. Hands are very important to primates, which use them not only for grasping and climbing but also for exploring. The fingertips, which are protected by nails, contain many nerve endings that make them very sensitive to texture. The presence of nails on fingers and toes is another feature unique to primates.

All primates have binocular vision, meaning that both eyes move together to focus on the same subject, because the eyes are at the front of the head rather than at the sides. These forward-facing eyes help primates to see in three dimensions and thus distinguish near objects from distant ones. Many other animals see in two dimensions only, with little or no depth perception. Primates can also see in color.

In all primates the brain is large in relation to body size. Humans have the largest, followed by the monkeys and apes, and then by the more primitive primates. The relative size of the brain is connected with intelligence and behavior. The apes are particularly intelligent non-human primates. Chimpanzees have been observed using tools in the wild, and have even been taught to communicate by using sign language or symbols.

Although the other non-human primates are not as intelligent as the apes, they all demonstrate quickly learned behavior, which means behavior patterns observed and copied from others. Young primates grow and mature slowly, which gives them a long time to observe and learn skills from their mothers and other members of their group.

All the features that man shares with the non-human primates, such as grasping hands and three-dimensional color vision, are useful for tree-living. These characteristics, together with the fact that the great majority of modern primates live in the trees, suggests that the earliest ancestors of human beings also lived in this environment. If that was true, human evolution began with a descent from the trees, and in fact the features that were necessary for tree life were the very ones that laid the foundation for success on the ground.

Individual species representing the major modern groups of non-human primates, are shown in the picture opposite. The number by the picture of each species corresponds to the same number on the map and shows where each species lives. Non-human primates are found throughout the world between latitudes 30° north and south of the Equator. Only the macaques of Japan live naturally outside these limits.

1 White-handed gibbon
Hylobates lar

2 Moholi bushbaby
Galago moholi

3 Red-mantled tamarin
Saguinus illigeri

4 Bornean proboscis monkey
Nasalis larvatus

5 Slow loris
Nycticebus coucang

6 Blue monkey
Ceropithecus mitis

7 Ringtailed lemur
Lemur catta

8 Chimpanzee
Pan troglodytes

9 Verreaux's sifaka
Propithecus verreauxi

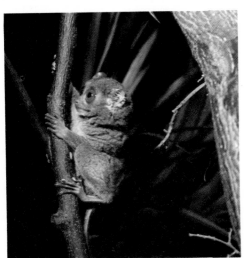

10 Philippine tarsier
Tarsius syrichta

11 Red howler monkey
Alouatta sunfeniculus

Myth and Religion

Throughout history man has recognized the similarities between himself and the non-human primates, although the relationship has been variously interpreted in different parts of the world. The myths and religions of many peoples express a close affinity between humans and the animal world. Many gods were given the attributes of animals, including the non-human primates – for example, in ancient Egypt the god Thoth was often portrayed as a baboon. In India today, Hindus hold the monkey god Hanuman sacred as the ally of the legendary hero Rama. In a few areas of the world there is a close connection, in creation myths, between monkeys or apes and humans. On the island of Sulawesi in Indonesia, for example, the inhabitants trace their ancestry directly to the island's local black ape.

Western cultures, however, relegated apes and monkeys to a less respectable position, basing their beliefs on the Old Testament account of the Creation. According to this, man, formed in the image of God, was believed to have dominion over the animal world. The gulf between man and animals was further widened both by the knowledge of good and evil acquired by Adam and Eve in the Garden of Eden, and the belief that man has a soul. Apes and monkeys were popularly portrayed as imperfect reflections of human beings, with animal minds in human-like bodies. They were often used to symbolize sin.

Western philosophers and historians, particularly in the seventeenth and eighteenth centuries, likened the variety of forms of life to a ladder. Each rung or step on the ladder was occupied by similar forms of life and each higher step by slightly more complex forms. This was called the Scale of Nature, or the Chain of Being. It extended from minerals through the lower forms of life to human beings and beyond to the angels. Human beings stood closest to the angels, and the monkeys and apes stood closest to humans. There was no denial that a similarity in body form existed, but the human ability to think and understand, and particularly the idea of the spiritual human soul, drew the boundary between civilized man and the animal world.

The Chain of Being was not an evolutionary

The subject of Adam and Eve, shown here with some of the animals of God's creation in the Garden of Eden, was a popular one with artists for many centuries. Such paintings followed the view expressed in the Bible that God had created the world and everything in it in six days, and that nothing had changed or altered since. In the nineteenth century, however, the scientist Charles Darwin suggested that all living things have gradually evolved through time into their present forms.

The ancient Egyptian god Thoth (above), in the form of a baboon, is worshipping the sacred eye of the sun god Re. This scene was painted between 1085 BC and 945 BC.

A modern Hindu shrine in honor of the monkey god Hanuman, who is revered as a giver of strength and wisdom.

sequence. There was no direct connection between the steps of the ladder. The Chain of Being was meant to reveal the pattern of life, and more specifically the pattern of the Creation according to the Bible. Taking a biblical view, it was believed that no type of animal had changed in form since the Creation and that no type of animal had died out, or become extinct, since that time, except for those that had not been saved in Noah's ark.

These beliefs in divine creation, in the unchanging nature of animal types, and in the imperfect nature of apes and monkeys were obstacles to the acceptance of the idea of evolution. Nineteenth-century scientists, notably the British scientist Charles Darwin, saw the Chain of Being as an evolutionary sequence, which suggested a natural relationship between man and the primates. This was a revolutionary idea and met tremendous moral and scientific opposition.

Theories about Evolution

Charles Darwin (1809–82), the scientist who published a book on his theory of evolution in 1859.

Alfred Russell Wallace (1823–1913), another scientist who believed that all living things had evolved.

T. H. Huxley (1825–95), was among the first scientists to suggest that man might have an apelike ancestor.

During the eighteenth century scientists began seriously to question the belief that no animal had changed in form since the Creation. The scientists knew that new varieties of plants and animals could be produced by selective breeding. In addition, more and more fossils were being discovered, many of which represented extinct animals.

In 1809 Jean-Baptiste de Lamarck, a French naturalist, proposed the first theory of evolution that caught public attention. Lamarck believed that all organisms achieve perfection of form through change. He thought that the effects of the environment on the parents' bodies could be inherited by their offspring. He called this process the inheritance of acquired characteristics. Lamarck's theory was not widely accepted because he provided little evidence to support it.

From 1831 to 1836 Charles Darwin traveled to different places on board a ship called the *Beagle*, studying natural history and collecting specimens. As a result, he put forward a theory of evolution by natural selection. He maintained that natural selection was based on three principles. Firstly, there was variation among animals or plants of the same type. Just as brothers and sisters differed in size, strength

or hair color, so did the members of any single species. Secondly, more offspring were born in each generation than could survive. Thirdly, those individuals that were best adapted to their environment lived to pass on their characteristics to the next generation. As the environment changed, new forms of life slowly developed from old ones.

Alfred Russell Wallace, a young British naturalist working in Indonesia, independently arrived at the same conclusions as Darwin. Wallace and Darwin presented a joint paper on the topic just before Darwin's influential book *The Origin of Species by Natural Selection* was published in 1859.

Darwin mentioned man only once in *The Origin of Species* (as his book is usually known): "Much light will be thrown on the origins of man and his history." From then on Darwin and scientists who accepted his ideas worked to establish the truth of human descent, not from the modern apes but from a common ancestor of the modern apes and man.

Among those scientists was the Englishman Thomas Henry Huxley, who published *Man's Place in Nature* in 1864. In it he demonstrated that man's body is more similar to that of the modern apes than the modern apes' bodies are to those of modern monkeys.

This historic photograph of excavations at Trinil, Java, was taken in 1900. Here, in the early 1890s, the Dutch doctor Eugène Dubois had found the fossil remains now called Java Man.

He argued that if natural selection were accepted as the process by which apes developed from monkeys, it could also be the process by which human beings developed from an apelike ancestor.

There was still very little fossil evidence to support the proposed evolutionary relationships between human beings and the other primates. The only known human fragments were those of Neanderthal Man, which had lived in Europe from about 150,000 to 34,000 years ago. However, in 1889 a young Dutch doctor, Eugène Dubois, went to southeast Asia in search of fossils of earlier man. He chose southeast Asia because it was the home of the orangutan – one of modern man's closest living relatives. In 1891 Dubois was successful and found the human fossils now known as Java Man, and so started the modern study of human evolution.

The revolutionary idea that man was closely related to the apes was a popular source of cartoons in the nineteenth century. In this one, Henry Bergh, the founder of the Society for the Prevention of Cruelty to Animals, tells Charles Darwin to stop insulting apes.

MR. BERGH TO THE RESCUE
THE DEFRAUDED GORILLA: *"That Man wants to claim my pedigree. He says he is one of my Descendants."*
MR. BERGH: *"Now, MR. DARWIN, how could you insult him so."*

Organizing the Evidence

Zoologists in the late nineteenth century worked out the evolutionary history of modern primates according to similarities and differences in body form. This principle still forms the basis of the modern system of naming and classifying living things. The system of classification used today was introduced in 1735 by a Swedish scientist called Carl von Linné, who is better known by the Latinized form of his name – Carolus Linnaeus. In the Linnaean system all forms of life, both animal and plant, are arranged in a hierarchy with all forms that are similar grouped together at each level.

Linnaeus had six levels in his hierarchy of animal life. At the bottom Linnaeus placed the species, which is a group of animals or plants that can breed with each other and produce fertile offspring. Similar species were grouped together into a genus, similar genera (the plural of genus) into an order, similar orders into a class, similar classes into a kingdom, and the kingdoms into an empire. The empire was the universal level of his hierarchy and also included minerals.

When Linnaeus introduced this system there were less than 5000 known species of animals. Today there are over a million. As a result, Linnaeus's system has been modified, and the modern hierarchy of animal life may have twenty or more levels of relationship.

Linnaeus called individual species by the names of both their species and genus groups. This system is called the system of binominal nomenclature (*bi* = two, *nomen* = name, *nomenclature* = system of names). The binominal name for humans is *Homo sapiens*: *Homo* is the name of the genus and *sapiens* the name of the species.

One of the chief criticisms of this classification system is that the species is the only kind of group in the hierarchy that actually exists in nature. Animals that can breed together and so belong to a single species are relatively easy to recognize. However, the groupings in the hierarchy above the species level depend for their definition not on their existence in nature but on the conclusions drawn from the study of their similarities and differences. Different taxonomists – scientists who classify forms of life – may draw different conclusions and as a result classify animals differently.

Classifying fossilized forms of life is much more difficult. Because fossils are not alive it is impossible to tell whether they could breed with each other, and therefore it is not certain which ones belong to the same species. Classification is also difficult because often all that scientists have to work with are teeth or fragments of bone.

As a result there is often confusion over fossil species and their names. The Linnaean system of classification was developed long before fossils were known and the theory of evolution accepted. Although it has been adapted for fossils, it is not completely suitable. Some fossil specimens have been known by three or four different Linnaean binominal names as scientific interpretations of their relationships have changed.

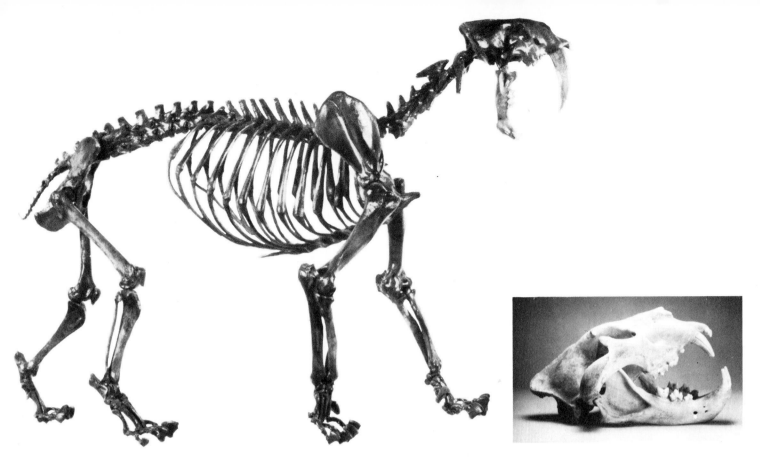

The skeleton of the saber-tooth (above) was assembled from bones found in the Rancho La Brea tar pits, California. Apparently the animals died when they blundered into the pits. Chemicals in the tar helped preserve the bones. Generally scientists find damaged specimens representing only one small part of an animal's body. Comparison with living species forms part of the process of classifying fossils. The basic similarity of the skulls of the lioness (above right) and the saber-tooth show they are quite closely related. (Both are in the same family, Felidae, which includes living and extinct cats.) Similarity of appearance does not always show a close biological relationship, so scientists use as many features as possible when classifying fossils. The relationship between the skeleton and body of the living lioness (below right) also helps in the reconstruction of the saber-tooth (below left).

How Fossils are Formed

Evolutionary trees for modern primates, which can be constructed simply on the basis of the similarities and differences among them, can show the general branching pattern of animal evolution. However, they cannot give the date when the evolutionary branches separated from each other. Nor can they say anything about the extinct animals that make up these evolutionary lines. And they cannot explain what these animals looked like, or when or under what environmental conditions they existed. Only the fossils themselves can reveal this information.

Bones and teeth found as fossils do not have the same chemical composition as they had at the death of the animal. During the thousands or millions of years that they have been buried in the earth the chemicals in the bone or tooth have been replaced by minerals from the ground – most often silica or calcium. This process is called replacement and through it the original structure of the bone or tooth is accurately preserved.

Fossils can also occur as molds, trails, or casts. A mold is an impression of an animal or plant left in the earth or rock in which it was buried. Molds of shells and other small, simple forms of life are quite common. Fossil trails, tracks, or footprints of primates and humans are rare, although a wonderfully preserved series of footprints was discovered in Tanzania in 1978–9.

The most frequently found type of cast of primate and human fossils is an endocranial cast, a cast of the cavity that houses the brain. Endocranial casts are formed when the brain decomposes and the cavity fills up with fine sediments that then harden into stone. Although this type of cast is only of the inside of the skull and not of the brain itself, it usually records the major structural features of the surface of the brain.

In 1924, the first African hominid fossil thought to be more than a million years old was discovered by Professor Raymond Dart, an Englishman working in South Africa. The fossil, named Taung after the site where it was found, included an endocranial cast, facial bones, jaw bones and a complete set of baby teeth. From his knowledge of human skulls, Dart recognized that the endocranial cast belonged to a hominid and not an ape.

Excavating can be delicate, tricky work. This paleontologist is using a paintbrush to remove soil from around the shoulder-blade of a hoofed animal, at Bacon Hole, a site on the Gower Peninsula, in South Wales, Britain.

Fossilization is a chancy process. The sediments in which the casts, molds, or trails are found need to solidify rapidly for fossilization to take place. For bones and teeth to be fossilized, the animal has to be buried very soon after death in deposits that slow down decomposition and encourage mineral replacement.

Finding fossils also involves chance. The deposits in which the fossils are buried must be close enough to the present-day ground surface to be accessible. Erosion of the ground surface or geological movement, such as uplift of the earth's crust, or both, can bring long-buried fossils near the surface.

These casts of human brain cavities, called endocranial casts by scientists, were found at the South African cave site of Swartkrans in 1936. The cast in the center right of the picture is shown together with the part of the skull to which it belongs.

The diagrams below show how the cave deposits at Swartkrans were probably formed. Many hominid remains have been found at this site, which is thought to be about two million years old.

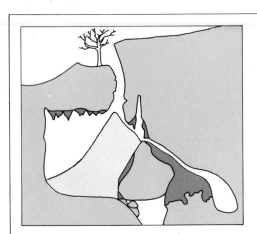

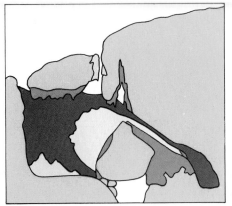

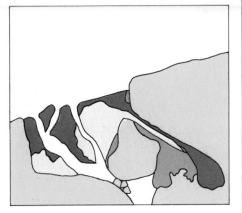

A deep shaft in the dolomite opened into an underground cave. Soil, rocks and bones fell into the cave, and over many millions of years hardened into another type of rock.

In time, the original shaft became blocked, and the cave roof collapsed. Another shaft opened. Rocks and soil fell down it and hardened into breccia, a cement-like rock.

Slowly the ground was eroded until the younger breccia was exposed. The process of erosion continues, allowing recovery of the original fossilized bones.

 Dolomite – a type of limestone

 Travertine – a hard limestone Old breccia formed from soil and rock pieces

 Younger breccia

17

What Fossils Show

These four illustrations show how scientists reconstruct a prehistoric hominid from a few skull fragments. First, surviving pieces are put into shape and plaster is substituted for the missing bits (1). Muscles that would be attached to such bones are added (2 and 3). Hair and skin (4) give as complete a picture as possible based on the available evidence.

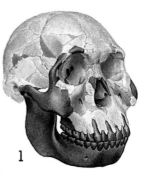

Physical anthropologists can tell a great deal about an extinct animal from a small fragment of fossil bone or a few teeth. Studying the bones and teeth can give a picture of man's ancestors, for example what they may have looked like and eaten. These deductions are based primarily on the comparison of the fossil specimens with their modern counterparts. For example, a small bone (the terminal phalanx) from

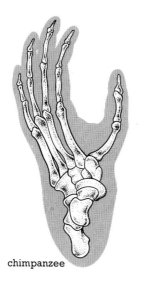

chimpanzee   human

The two illustrations above show the differences between the skeleton and shape of the foot (in gray) of a chimpanzee and that of a human. In particular note the position and shape of the big toe. A fossil of the tiny bone from the tip of a big toe was found at Olduvai Gorge, in East Africa. Its thick, slightly twisted shape confirmed it as hominid; chimpanzees and other apes have a straight, tapered toe bone.

the end of the big toe of an early hominid was found at Olduvai Gorge in Tanzania, East Africa, in 1961. By comparing this bone with toe bones from human and non-human primates, anthropologists concluded that the hominid to whom the bone belonged 1.5 million years ago walked upright on two legs.

When humans walk, the weight of the body goes first onto the heel, then along the outer edge of the foot, across the ball of the foot and finally to the big toe. Scientists call this the three-point walk. At the end of each step humans push off with the big toe, and in so doing twist the foot slightly outward. This twisting motion is reflected in the shape of the terminal phalanx, which is slightly twisted. No primate that walks on four legs has big toe bones like this.

The terminal phalanx is only one small clue to the way early hominids moved. The shape and fit of fossils of feet and leg bones, and the vertebrae of the backbone confirm that walking on two legs was one of the earliest human features to develop.

In many respects, however, early hominids looked more like non-human primates, such as present-day apes, than like human beings. One type of early hominid, which lived between two and one million years ago in East Africa, called *Australopithecus boisei* (*Australis* = southern, *pithecus* = ape, *boisei* after the Boise Foundation, which funded the excavations) has a skull which looks more like that of a gorilla than that of a hominid. The brain is small, and the face, jaws, and teeth are very large. There is also a crest of bone running along the top of the head to which the temporalis muscle, one of the main muscles that move the jaw, is attached. However, this crest of bone is nearer the front of the skull than it is in the gorilla which suggests that the hominid moved its jaw

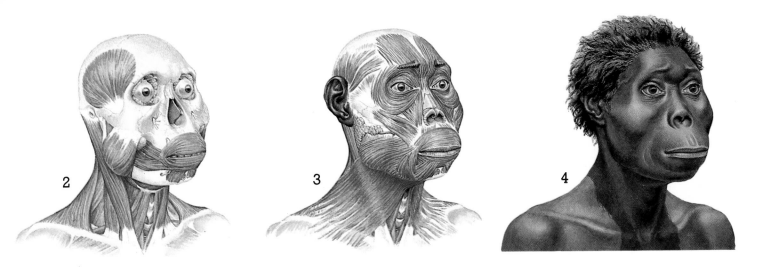

2

3

4

more like a man than like a gorilla.

In the gorilla the temporalis muscle pulls back toward the skull crest at an angle to the jaw, imparting the most strength at the front teeth for tearing and shearing. But in the hominid, the muscle would pull almost straight up to the crest, exerting the strongest force on the back teeth for more efficient grinding. Humans do not have a skull crest, because the human cranium is so high that the temporalis muscle attaches to the side rather than the top of the skull. Otherwise the human temporalis works in a similar way to the early hominid's. The form of the hominid's teeth – particularly the small canines (which permit side to side chewing) and the thick enamel on the molars (which protects the teeth from harsh foodstuffs) also suggests that this hominid was closer to modern man than to modern apes.

These drawings of the skulls of a modern gorilla, Australopithecus boisei *(a long extinct hominid) and a modern human (*Homo sapiens*) show some of the points scientists look for when trying to decide how ancient hominid fossils fit into the story of man's evolution. The gorilla has a large crest along the top of its skull, to which its jaw muscles are attached.* Australopithecus boisei *also has a skull crest, but it is much smaller and farther forward than the gorilla's. Modern humans have no crest.* Australopithecus boisei *has a flatter face and much smaller canine teeth than a gorilla, characteristics it shares with human beings.*

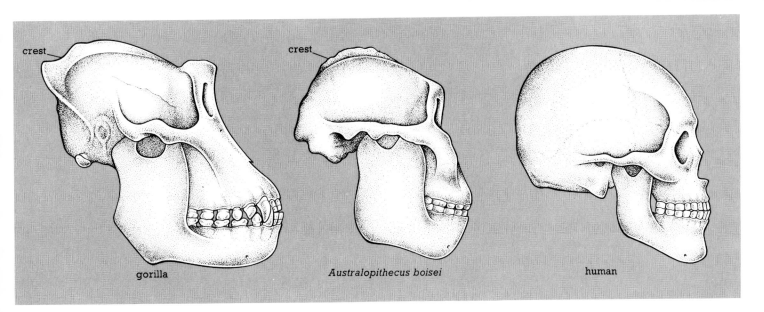

crest

crest

gorilla

Australopithecus boisei

human

How Fossils are Dated

To find the dates of plant and animal fossils, researchers turn to geochronology, the science of dating events in the earth's history. There are two major groups of geochronological techniques. One is absolute dating, which provides the age of a fossil or the deposits in which it is found. The other is relative dating, which measures the age of fossils or deposits in relation to other fossils or deposits. Relative dating can determine only whether a specific deposit or fossil is older than, younger than, or of the same period as another fossil or deposit. But such dating is useful because many fossil sites lack material that can be dated by absolute means.

The majority of the absolute dating techniques are based on radioactive decay. Because certain radioactive elements, such as uranium, thorium, or radioactive forms of other elements, such as potassium 40 or carbon 14, decay at a specific rate, the decay can be used like a clock. Scientists measure how much decay has taken place to find out the absolute age of a specific sample.

Dating by carbon 14 or radiocarbon is perhaps the best-known absolute dating technique. Carbon 14 makes up a small proportion of all the carbon in living matter. Therefore scientists can date anything that has been alive, such as charcoal, wood, peat, and bone, by measuring how much the carbon 14 has decayed.

However, carbon 14 dating can only be used on finds of up to 50,000–70,000 years of age. Since the fossil record for human evolution may extend back 8 million years or more, carbon 14 dating is useful only to determine ages for the comparitively recent stages of evolution.

Other absolute techniques provide dates for the rock deposits in which the fossils are found rather than for the fossils themselves. These techniques include potassium-argon dating, uranium series dating, and fission track dating. For any of these techniques to be successful it is essential that the rock was

The layers of rock or strata on the west of Lake Turkana, Kenya, show clearly in this photograph. Many hominid remains have been found in the area and their relation to the different layers of strata is a useful aid in dating them.

Scientists working on a potassium-argon dating test in a laboratory at the University of California at Berkeley, where this dating method was first developed in the 1950s.

formed at or near the time the fossils were deposited. Furthermore the rock must be of volcanic origin, for instance lava. However, there are only a few areas in the world, among them East Africa, where human or non-human primate fossils have been found with volcanic rocks either above or below them.

For sites that lack volcanic rock or are beyond the range of carbon 14 dating, relative dating techniques have to be used. The two most important of these techniques are biostratigraphy and paleomagnetism.

Biostratigraphy is the study of the groups of fossil animals found in different strata of rock. By comparing fossils from one area where absolute dates are unknown with an area that has a known absolute date, it is often possible to determine the approximate age of the undated area.

Paleomagnetic dating uses the reversals that have occurred in the earth's magnetic field as a yardstick against which to determine the relative age of mineral deposits. Throughout geological history the direction of the earth's magnetic field has reversed many times. These changes, which were reflected in mineral deposits accumulating at the time, can be discovered by studying the direction of the deposit's magnetic particles. The resulting data can be compared with that from other sites to establish the relative ages, or even the absolute age, if identical data has been absolutely dated at other sites.

Time and Primate Evolution

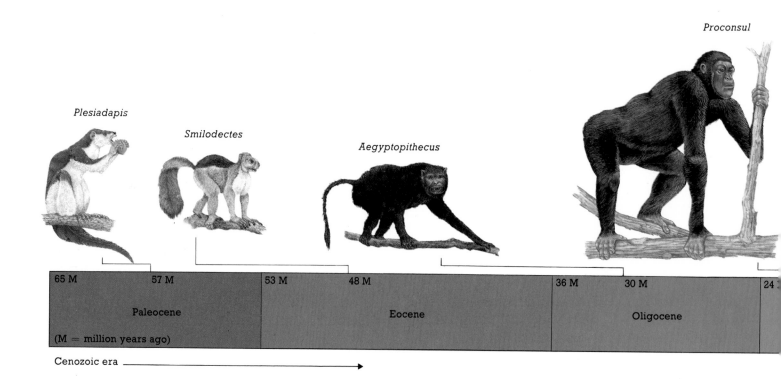

Plesiadapis

Smilodectes

Aegyptopithecus

Proconsul

65 M	57 M	53 M	48 M	36 M	30 M	24

Paleocene

Eocene

Oligocene

(M = million years ago)

Cenozoic era ⟶

The primate evolutionary story extends back in time over 65 million years to the end of the geological era known as the Mesozoic. During the Mesozoic the dinosaurs were dominant and the mammals, the warm-blooded animals, were slowly evolving. Among the mammals were the ancestors of primates.

The earliest known fossil believed to be of a primitive primate is a tooth dating from the end of the Mesozoic era that was found in eastern Montana. The fossil is called *Purgatorius ceratops*: *Purgatorius* from Purgatory Hill where it was found, and *ceratops* because it was found in the same stream channel as a fossil of the dinosaur *Triceratops*.

The development of the rest of the primate line

occurred during the subsequent 65,000,000-year era – the Cenozoic era – which is divided into seven epochs. From the earliest to the most recent, these are the Paleocene, Eocene, Oligocene, Miocene, Pliocene, and the Recent, or Holocene. The earlier Paleocene primates possessed only a few of the features found in living primates, such as the structure of the ear region of the skull and the structure of the molar teeth.

By Eocene times, however, the primates had become more like the modern primitive primates, the lemurs, lorises, and bushbabies, and another small primate, the tarsier, that lives today in the forests of southeast Asia. Although the tarsier looks

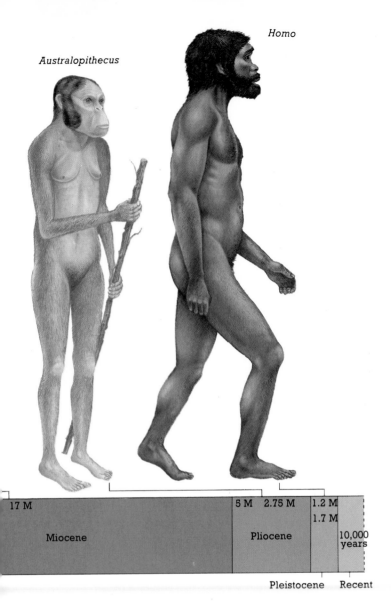

Australopithecus

Homo

17 M

Miocene

5 M 2.75 M

Pliocene

1.2 M

1.7 M

10,000
years

Pleistocene   Recent

Primates typical of each of the seven epochs into which scientists divide the Cenozoic are shown here. The abbreviated dates refer to approximately when each epoch began and when each primate lived. All the creatures are drawn in proportion to each other. The primates shown (named only by genus) are from left to right: Plesiadapis, *a rodent-like primate from France;* Smilodecties, *a lemur-like primate from North America;* Aegyptopithecus, *a more advanced primate from the Fayum, a fossil-rich area of desert in Egypt;* Proconsul, *an early ape from East Africa;* Australopithecus, *a hominid from Africa; and* Homo, *a hominid of the genus that includes man and his immediate ancestors.*

rather like the primitive primates it shares a more recent common ancestor with the apes and the monkeys than with the lemurs and the lorises.

Most scientists divide the Eocene primates into two main groups, the Adapidae and the Omonyidae. The Adapidae are thought to be the ancestors of most of the modern primitive primates, while the Omonyidae are, broadly speaking, the ancestors of the modern tarsiers, monkeys, apes, and humans.

The first traces of more advanced primates appear in the Oligocene era, which began about 36 million years ago. Although the primates living at this time did not look exactly like modern monkeys or apes, fossils of their skulls and teeth show that they may

represent the ancestors of these higher primates.

By the Miocene, the apes were clearly separate from the monkeys of Africa and Asia, and the story of human evolution may have started as early as the middle of the Miocene epoch, about 16 million years ago. From this time scientists have found fossil teeth and some fragments of jaw that are similar to the teeth and jaws of later hominids. As yet no fossil skulls or skeletons of these Miocene primates have been found, but because the teeth and jaw fragments are of broadly human form these fossils may be at the very root of hominid evolution.

By about four million years ago, the human line was definitely separate from the line leading to the modern apes. From the fossil evidence Pliocene hominids clearly walked on two legs, and their jaws and teeth were human rather than apelike. By the end of the Pliocene epoch and the beginning of the Pleistocene there is good evidence that the hominid brain had begun to expand, and that these early hominids were also beginning to use tools. However, from the known fossil evidence, hominids of modern form did not appear until 100,000 years ago.

The Miocene World

In the Oligocene and Early Miocene epochs the geography of Africa, Europe and Asia was very different from today. The land surface was much flatter, and Africa was completely separated from Europe and Asia by a vast sea – the Tethys Sea.

Geologists now know that the continents move in relationship to one another and that about 18 million years ago Africa collided with Eurasia. A landbridge was formed between the Arabian peninsula, which was part of Africa at this time, and the Middle East. There may also have been a land connection between North Africa and Italy, or between Morocco and Spain at Gibraltar.

The landbridges then resulted in an exchange of animals between the two continents. African animals, including the apes and monkeys, spread from Africa into Europe and Asia. At the same time, Eurasian animals, such as some rodents and cats, entered Africa.

The movement of the continents was also accompanied by a change in the climate. Although the world's climate had been steadily cooling since the Eocene epoch, the trend increased during the Miocene. By the Late Miocene the Eurasian climate was also drier and had more marked seasons.

The Miocene was also a period of mountain building. When the continents collided, the resulting pressure pushed up and buckled the land surface, producing mountains. The Pyrenees between France and Spain, the Swiss Alps, the Zagros Mountains of Iran, and the Himalayas were all being formed during this time.

The changed climate presented previously tropical animals – including the apes – with new environments to which they had to adapt. Middle and Late Miocene fossil apes from Eurasia are found in environments ranging from humid rain forests, through temperate woodlands, to grassland.

The climate was also changing in Africa. During the Middle Miocene, 16 to 11 million years ago, the mountains and huge rift valleys of East Africa were forming. The high mountains produced rain-shadow areas – areas of low rainfall – which resulted in the spread of grasslands in Africa as well as in Eurasia. From these environments have come fossilized teeth and fragments of jaws that resemble those of the hominids more closely than any previous fossils.

The spread of the grasslands had some marked effects on the animals. From the Miocene, many fossil animals of present-day form begin to appear. During

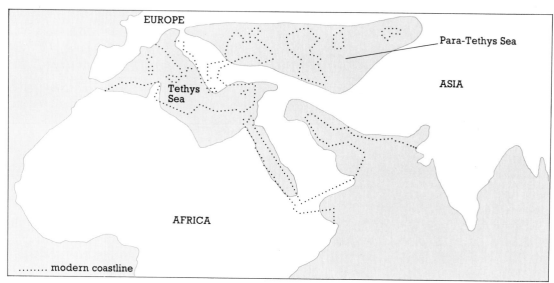

The Tethys Sea, once a vast ocean which separated Africa from Europe and Asia, is shown here as it looked about 16 million years ago – about two million years after a series of movements in the earth's crust connected the land masses of Africa and Eurasia. The extensive inland arm of the Tethys is known as the Para-Tethys Sea.

A view across part of the great African Rift valley in Kenya; in the distance is Mount Longonot, an extinct volcano. This valley was formed during the geological upheavals of the Miocene epoch.

Ancestors of antelopes similar to these African impala (below) had to adapt to eating grass during the Miocene epoch, because tropical forest could no longer survive in the increasingly dry climate.

the Early Miocene, for example, hoofed animals such as the horse and antelope were primarily leaf-eaters. However, with the spread of the grasslands they had to adapt to the new conditions and become grass-eaters. Their teeth became high crowned (long from the chewing surface to the root) to chew the harsh grasses that were now their food. Their legs became longer, with fewer toes, so that they could move faster to escape from predators on the open grasslands.

Since the climatic and environmental changes of the Middle and the Late Miocene produced such marked changes in these animals, it is possible that these same changes triggered the emergence of man.

Who is Man's Ancestor?

On an expedition in the Siwalik Hills of Kashmir during 1931–2, a young Yale University graduate student, G. E. Lewis, collected a few jaw fragments that he considered belonged to the earliest distinct members of the hominid line. He believed that the pieces showed the basic human dental features of a short, relatively flat face, small canine teeth, and no diastema – the space in the upper jaw between the canine and the incisor teeth, to receive a larger lower canine tooth. Lewis called this creature *Ramapithecus* (*Rama* = a Hindu god, *pithecus* = ape). But Lewis's claims were rejected by scientists.

In 1960s the American geologist and authority on Miocene apes, Elwyn Simons, reexamined the fossil collection from the Siwalik Hills and confirmed Lewis's claim. About the same time, other *Ramapithecus* fragments were found at a site at Fort Ternan in Kenya. These ramapithecines were about 14 million years old – two million years older than those Lewis had found.

Because of the age of these African specimens, most Western scientists were ready to agree that *Ramapithecus* was the logical ancestor of man – and that Africa was the cradle of mankind.

Over the years other lines of analysis, as well as new fossil discoveries, have challenged this conclusion. The so-called molecular approach has offered the most serious challenge. First put forward by a Cambridge biology professor named George Nuttall, the method was based on the knowledge that when blood serum from one animal is injected into a second animal, the second produces antibodies against the protein in the serum. When serum from the second animal is combined with serum from a third, the antibodies combine with the similar proteins in that serum to form a reaction. The greater the reaction, the closer the relationship between the first and third animals.

Over the past decade the molecular approach has been greatly expanded and refined. Several different approaches – often called genetic measurements – have been explored. Two Americans, biochemist Alan Wilson and chemist Vincent Sarich, working at the University of California in Berkeley use a process called protein sequencing to measure the difference in proteins between species. They have concluded that man, chimpanzee and gorilla shared a single ancestor as recently as five million years ago. Other

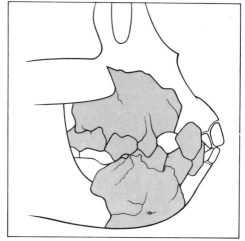

These pieces of Ramapithecus *(right) were found at Fort Ternan in Kenya and date to about 14 million years ago. In the photograph the large front tooth is on the right. The drawing (far right) is a reconstruction to show how the pieces of jaw would fit if the creature were alive.*

processes measure the basic genetic material, known as DNA, and compare the DNA of different living species. Tests involving man and chimpanzee show that about 99 per cent of their DNA is identical.

Some scientists question the assumption basic to all the molecular approaches – that molecular change happens at a constant rate. A number of anthropologists still insist on limiting the search for man's origins to the fossil record.

Although controversy continues to surround the molecular procedures, all of the methods – including Nuttall's original one – indicate that the evolutionary split between man and the apes came after the date of the *Ramapithecus* fossils.

In the 1970s the hominid status of *Ramapithecus* was challenged on the basis of the fossils themselves. The Siwalik rocks and fossils were re-dated and are now considered by some geologists to be between 12 and 8 million years old. The Fort Ternan finds were reanalyzed and new and more complete *Ramapithecus* fossils were discovered in Pakistan and Turkey. These fossils, however, had apelike traits – the lower jaws were narrow, the upper incisors slanted forward, and there was a diastema. Other possible *Ramapithecus* fossils have been found in China and Hungary, but their classification is not yet certain.

Fossils discovered in the Siwalik Hills (above) of Kashmir, India, in the 1930s were the first to be named Ramapithecus. *The fossils are considered the remains of a very remote human ancestor by some experts.*

The map (below) shows where Ramapithecus *fossils have been found. The sites date from about 16 to 8 million years ago, and indicate a wide area of habitation.*

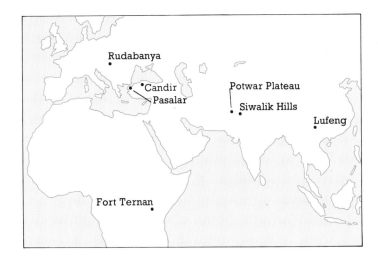

Ramapithecus in Controversy

The validity – if any – of *Ramapithecus*'s place in human evolution depends on the similarities firstly between *Ramapithecus* and modern human beings, and secondly between *Ramapithecus* and the other Miocene fossil apes.

When compared with humans and modern apes, *Ramapithecus* possesses distinctly hominid facial and dental characteristics. Its face is short and deep, and its canine teeth are relatively small. Recent analysis has also shown that its tooth enamel is thick, and its molars are more human-like than apelike in form. Some scientists, therefore, believe that these characteristics place *Ramapithecus* in the hominid line.

However, there is much controversy over which fossils belong to *Ramapithecus* and which are just small specimens of another Miocene creature widespread in Europe and Asia called *Sivapithecus*. The apes named *Sivapithecus* (*Siva* = a Hindu god), also have thick tooth enamel and molars similar to *Ramapithecus*. In fact the only way molars of the smaller *Ramapithecus* and the larger *Sivapithecus* can be clearly distinguished is by the difference in size. As a result, other scientists classify *Ramapithecus* with these Miocene fossil apes and believe that it is not a hominid.

A few fossil limb bones that may belong to *Ramapithecus* have been found in the Potwar Plateau region of Pakistan. These bones indicate that whatever classification the creature eventually receives, it did not walk upright as hominids did.

The only general conclusion scientists are ready to make is that all the Miocene primates with thickly enameled teeth were probably adapting to the climatic changes and dietary opportunities in the Miocene in a similar way.

Although *Ramapithecus* may not have been a hominid, many scientists believe that it is the most likely of the apes of the Miocene with thick tooth enamel to have been the ancestor of the hominids. For the present, however, the proper role for *Ramapithecus* in the drama of man's origins is still uncertain.

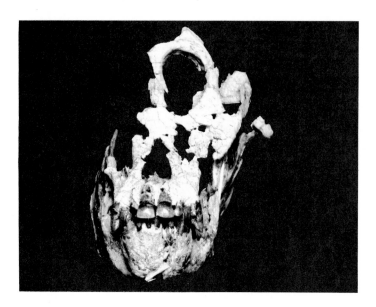

The remains of Sivapithecus indicus *(above left) show the large face of this Miocene primate who lived at about the same time as* Ramapithecus. *The skull (in gray at left) is similar in size to that of an orangutan (outlined in black).*

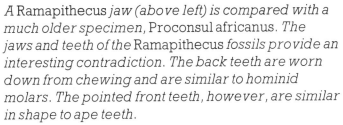
A Ramapithecus *jaw (above left) is compared with a much older specimen,* Proconsul africanus. *The jaws and teeth of the* Ramapithecus *fossils provide an interesting contradiction. The back teeth are worn down from chewing and are similar to hominid molars. The pointed front teeth, however, are similar in shape to ape teeth.*

This reconstruction of a ramapithecine family (left) shows them collecting food. In open woodland and grassland habitats such as this, they probably ate small items such as berries. The looks and habits of Ramapithecus *are based on very limited evidence, as most Miocene fossils consist only of jaws and teeth, often in poor condition.*

The Four Million Year Gap

The Miocene – that span of time from roughly 24 million to 5 million years ago – has been called the age of the apes. In Africa, Europe and Asia the fossil evidence indicates that apes were probably the dominant form of primate, living successfully in both forested and more open environments. However, by about eight million years ago, the Miocene apes seem to have disappeared almost completely. Scientists are still trying to work out the appropriate ancestry for the apes alive today. In fact, the fossil record for apes after eight million years is distressingly empty.

Although climate and environmental changes taking place toward the end of the Miocene probably account for the disappearance of the ancient apes, most anthropologists admit that there must have been other factors at work as well. However, the dearth of ape fossils after eight million years makes it hard to come up with other valid explanations.

In fact, between eight million years and four million years ago, next to no fossils relevant to the evolution of either apes or humans have been recovered. Most anthropologists refer to this period as the gap. The few key finds from this period come from Kenya and, most recently, Libya. There is a single tooth from Lukeino, Kenya, that has been dated at 6.5 million years. A small fragment of a jaw with a single tooth found at Lothagam, Kenya, dates to 5.5 million years ago. A temporal bone (from the side of the head) also from Kenya may be as old as 4.5 million years. And a piece of the humerus (the upper arm bone near the elbow) from Kanapoi is about four million years old.

Three fragmentary fossils from Sahabi, Libya – a piece of a collarbone, a skull section and a lower leg bone – have been called hominid. Found during 1979 and 1981, these fragments have been dated as between seven and five million years old. Although the Libyan fossils are still being studied, the leg bone fragment appears to resemble those from upright-walking hominids.

Although anthropologists today are more cautious

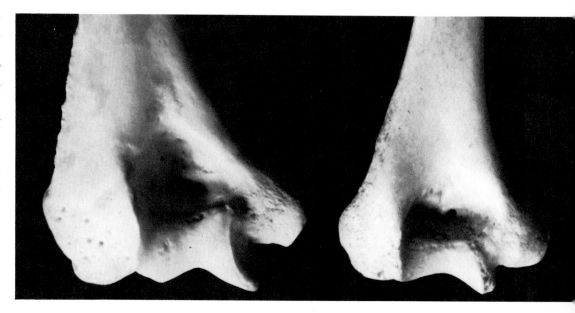

A comparison of the elbows of a chimpanzee (right), a modern human (center) and the fossil fragment of an elbow joint (far right) from Kanapoi, Kenya, suggests that the fossil is possibly from an early bipedal hominid. Analysis of the bone's surface-to-weight ratios indicates that like the modern human elbow, but unlike the chimpanzee's elbow, it was not designed to support body weight.

This hominid jaw (right) found at Lothagam in Kenya contains a single tooth.

The Lukeino tooth (above) from Kenya has rounded upper surfaces and thick enamel, which would help the chewing of tough foods. Although it has these hominid characteristics, recent studies now question this status.

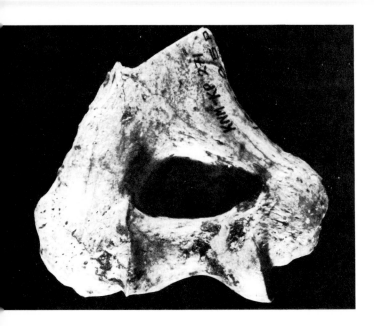

about classifying isolated fossils, this has not always been the case. The tooth found at Lukeino and pronounced hominid has recently been reexamined and compared with other specimens. It is now considered, in its shape and proportions, to be almost identical to that of a present-day chimpanzee.

In any event, the Lukeino tooth and the one found with the Lothagam jaw fragment indicate no more than the fact that primates with thickly enameled teeth continued to live in East Africa during this period.

The piece of the arm bone from Kanapoi, however, is more informative. Experts have decided that this bone is unlike that of any quadrapedal (four-footed) primate. It is not designed to support body weight and, therefore, must have come from a bipedal creature.

The First Hominid Footprints

In 1977 the British archaeologist Mary Leakey and her team of fossil hunters announced a find that proved that man's ancestors were walking in the upright human fashion as early as 3.75 to 3.6 million years ago. At Laetoli, which lies south of Olduvai Gorge in northern Tanzania, Leakey and her group found not fossil bones but fossilized footprints.

Hominids, along with hares, antelopes and elephants, had walked across a plain that had been covered with a layer of volcanic ash from an eruption of Mount Sadiman, a nearby volcano. The ash, apparently, was slightly wet from a light rain shower and soft enough to leave clear outlines of the footprints of the passing animals. The ash dried, hardening into a cement-like layer, perfectly preserving the impressions.

The trails of the early hominids were immediately recognizable, for their footprints were almost identical to modern man's. The big toe was short and close to the other toes, rather than long and separate from them as in the grasping feet of the non-human primates. In addition, there was a clear arch, as in modern human feet.

The Laetoli prints show that there were three hominids walking close to each other, and possibly in single file. One set of footprints is large, one slightly smaller, and one smaller still. Perhaps these were the footprints of a family group, but this unique glimpse of man's early ancestors says little more about them. The footprints show that the hominids took small steps. This could be either because they were walking slowly or because they had short legs.

From studying the way primates move, and from looking at their bones and muscles, man's primate ancestors probably climbed and moved in the trees in a slow, deliberate fashion, as do some of the forest monkeys of South and Central America today. Adaptations useful for climbing – such as a tendency toward upright posture, short, rigid backs, broad chests and flexible joints – are found today not only in man but

One of the fossilized footprints found at Laetoli, Tanzania (right), photographed using the technique for measuring depth contours known as photogrammetry. The contours of both the Laetoli footprint (center right) and a modern human print (far right) show the same pattern of weight distribution in walking. The darkest colors, the dark brown and blue areas, show where the foot pressed most deeply into the ground. The lightest colors indicate where there was least pressure on the foot and so the print is shallow.

 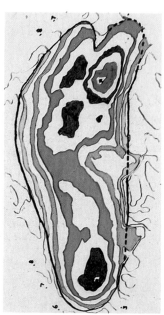 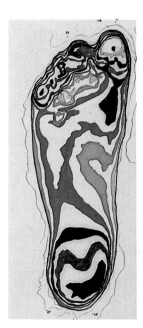

Mary Leakey sitting to the left of the incredible trail of fossilized hominid footprints found by her team at Laetoli. The large footprints were in fact made by two individuals; the second hominid, who had smaller feet, stepped precisely in the steps of the first. A set of much smaller footprints runs beside this trail. The trail of prints near Mary Leakey's right hand were made by an extinct type of horse.

also in the great apes. Such adaptations would have enabled the early hominids to develop bipedal walking with a minimum of evolutionary change to the skeletons. The changes that occurred included the loss of the grasping big toe and changes in the shape of the hipbone.

The spread of the graslands of Europe, Africa, and Asia in the Middle and Late Miocene would have provided new habitats and additional food sources for a creature who was not totally dependent on a life in or near trees. Did man's ancestors develop bipedal walking in order to inhabit the grasslands? These are questions the fossil record can not answer. Some anthropologists speculate that bipedal walking was originally for protection. Standing upright would raise the level of the eyes and therefore extend the range of vision to locate predators at a greater distance. Other scientists believe bipedalism developed because it freed the hands so that plant foods or tools could be carried back to the females and infants.

A Skeleton called Lucy

In 1973 the American anthropologist Donald Johanson and a team of scientists from the United States, France, and Ethiopia began a series of remarkable fossil discoveries from a number of sites collectively called Hadar, in the Afar area of Ethiopia. These fossils, together with the Laetoli footprints and fossils, are dated between about 4 and 3.2 million years old.

The key Hadar find, made in 1974, was a skeleton that was forty per cent complete, more complete than any previously found Pliocene skeleton. Research on the dating continues, but it is currently thought to be between 3.4 and 3 million years. It is rare to find so much of one fossil skeleton. Therefore many scientists want to study this one in order to reconstruct a better picture of the hominid as it existed when alive. The structure of the hipbones suggests that it was a female. From the length and weight of other bones, experts have concluded that she was about three and a half to four feet tall, and weighed only about sixty pounds. Her legs, hips, and backbone are clearly adapted to bipedal walking.

Lucy, as she was nicknamed, shows what at least one ancestral hominid from the Pliocene was like. Then, in 1975, a group of fossils representing 13 individuals who may have lived slightly earlier than Lucy, were found at Hadar. These fossils were different from Lucy. Some of these fossils were larger, and there were differences in the size and shape of the upper and lower jaws. There are two generally accepted opinions about what these differences in body size and jaw shape mean. Some anthropologists, including Johanson, believe that the larger fossils represent the males and the smaller ones represent the females of a single species. These scientists place the Hadar and Laetoli fossils in the genus *Australopithecus*, and have named them as a new species, *Australopithecus afarensis* (from Afar, the area where the finds were made).

Other anthropologists, such as Mary Leakey, be-

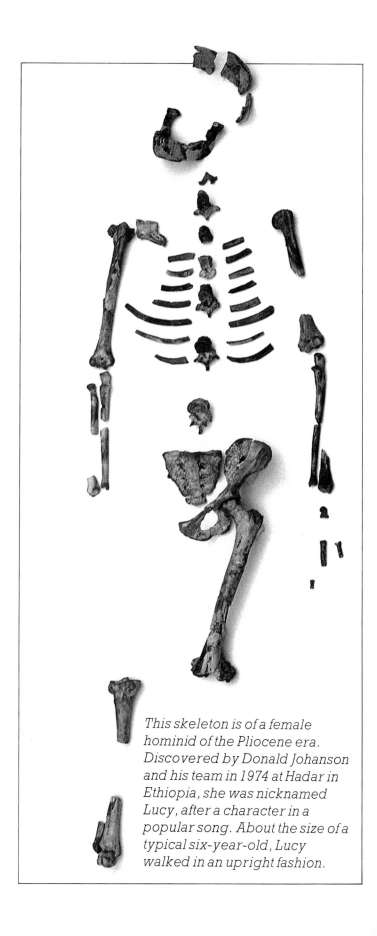

This skeleton is of a female hominid of the Pliocene era. Discovered by Donald Johanson and his team in 1974 at Hadar in Ethiopia, she was nicknamed Lucy, after a character in a popular song. About the size of a typical six-year-old, Lucy walked in an upright fashion.

Finding a fossil is an exciting moment for any excavator. Here Johanson triumphantly holds up a leg bone of a hominid found during work at Hadar.

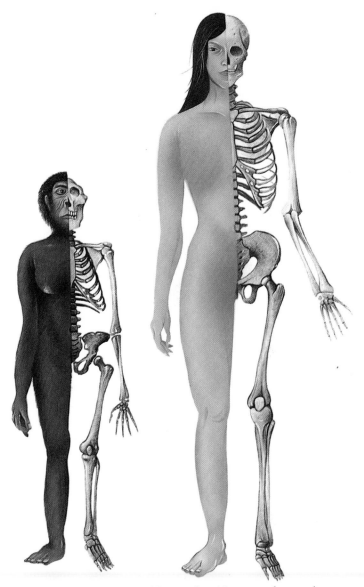

This reconstruction of Australopithecus afarensis *(above left) is based on Lucy. Comparison with the modern human suggests Lucy's size.*

lieve that these differences indicate not one but two species of hominid at Hadar. This is not impossible: fossils at other African sites show that between two and one million years ago there were quite clearly two different types of hominid living on the African savanna. These scientists generally classify Lucy, as well as similar small-bodied Hadar fossils, in the genus *Australopithecus*. They point out similarities to *Australopithecus africanus* (*africanus* = African), a type of hominid, represented by the Taung skull, that lived mainly in South Africa between about 3 and 2.5 million years ago. They classify the larger fossils from Hadar, as well as all the fossils from Laetoli, as early representatives of the genus *Homo*.

A final interpretation must await future fossil discoveries and further study of the fossils already excavated. However, the footprints at Laetoli and the fossils found at Hadar have provided some fascinating clues in the search for man's origins.

Finds from Olduvai

Olduvai Gorge is a stream-cut canyon in the eastern Serengeti Plain of northern Tanzania. It is about twenty-five miles long, and the eastern thirteen miles is rich in fossils. The gorge plunges three hundred feet at is deepest, and cuts through seven recognizable layers of deposits containing fossils. The deepest layer is about 1.9 million years old.

Olduvai is important for two main reasons. Firstly, beds, or layers, of sediment and volcanic ash occur between the deposits that contain the fossils. Because volcanic layers can be dated by potassium-argon and other absolute dating techniques the Olduvai finds can be dated accurately. Secondly, the deposits are undisturbed. There are remains of campsites and butchering-sites which provide important information about the hominids' lifestyle.

Fossils were first collected at Olduvai in 1913 by the German paleontologist Hans Reck. In 1925, Louis Leakey, the African-born son of English missionaries, saw Reck's fossil collection, and by 1931 Leakey had organized his own expedition to Olduvai. Over the next twenty-eight years he and his wife Mary, who joined the work in 1935, excavated at Olduvai when funds allowed. They recovered many animal fossils and stone tools, but found only two fragments of hominid skull and two hominid teeth.

However, the Leakeys' persistence paid off in 1959, when Mary Leakey discovered an almost complete skull of a large australopithecine. Louis Leakey originally named this skull *Zinjanthroups boisei*. *Zinj* is an Arabic name for East Africa, *anthropus* means human being, and *boisei* was for the person funding the work. This skull is still affectionately called "Zinj," but it is now considered by some anthropologists as *Australopithecus boisei*, a type of *Australopithecus*. It has been dated at about 1.75 million years old.

Apart from Zinj there are only a few other fossils at Olduvai that belong to the species *Australopithecus boisei*. Most of the Olduvai hominid fossils belong to

Louis Leakey photographed in front of a rockface at Olduvai Gorge, Tanzania, in 1965. In his right hand is the broken molar tooth of a dinotherium, a long extinct relative of the elephant. In the hat in his left hand is part of an elephant tooth that is a million years old.

a species known by some anthropologists as *Homo habilis* (handy man), who is considered to be the maker of the stone tools the Leakeys had found in the area. The *habilis* fossils had smaller, more human-like teeth than *Australopithecus boisei* and a larger brain in relation to their body size.

Homo habilis coexisted with *Australopithecus boisei* at Olduvai from 1.9–1.7 million years ago through to the period between 1.5 and 1.1 million years ago. The only fossil of *Australopithecus boisei* in these younger deposits is a tooth, but it is enough to show the presence of this hominid.

Although anthropologists disagree about the names used for the Olduvai fossils, most agree that the type represented by *boisei* became extinct by about one million years ago. They also believe that the *habilis* fossils evolved into another species of hominid, *Homo erectus* (upright man). This species, the direct ancestor of modern man, lived between 1.5 million and 300,000 years ago. In the younger deposits excavators found a well-preserved *Homo erectus* skull above the older *Homo habilis* material

It has a much larger braincase than *Homo habilis* and the skull is shaped differently. This *erectus* skull is long and low in relation to that of *Homo habilis*.

Other recent hominids have also been found at Olduvai. There are six fossils of the *Homo erectus* species that date from about 700,000 years ago. There is also the skeleton of *Homo sapiens* found by Hans Reck in 1913 that dates to only 17,000 years ago.

Although other more recently excavated African fossil sites have produced many more hominid fossils from the period spanning two million to one million years ago, the Olduvai stone tool discoveries are the most well documented in all Africa.

This view of Olduvai Gorge clearly shows a number of different layers or strata of rock. Thousands of hominid fossil fragments and stone tools have been recovered from this site by Mary and Louis Leakey.

Omo and Koobi Fora

Apart from Olduvai, other hominid sites outside South Africa being excavated in the 1960s were Yayo in Chad, Natron in Tanzania, Omo in Ethiopia, and Koobi Fora in Kenya. Yayo and Natron have each produced only single hominid fossils. Poorly preserved facial bones found at Yayo could be either those of an *Australopithecus* or an early *Homo*. A jaw unearthed at Natron is clearly *Australopithecus boisei*. However, the sites of Omo and at Koobi Fora have thrown more light on hominid evolution.

The fossil-bearing deposits of the Omo River reach a thickness of about 3500 feet and span the period between about 3.5 million and 0.8 million years ago. Over fifty thousand fossils have been found there since 1968 by an international team headed by the American anthropologist F. Clark Howell and the French anthropologist Yves Coppens. Most, however, are the remains of rats, pigs, antelopes and other animals. The hominid fossils – largely teeth and some bone fragments – number about 200. But, since the Omo fossils come from an area of intense volcanic activity, the entire fossil sequence has been extremely well-dated. The Omo animal fossils are being used to provide dates for other sites where similar fossils are found but absolute dating is not possible.

The fossil-rich deposits at Koobi Fora are on the dry eastern shore of Lake Turkana in northern Kenya. These deposits were excavated by Richard Leakey, the son of Louis and Mary Leakey. Richard Leakey's team found fossils of skulls, jaws, teeth and many other parts of skeletons. These bones are better preserved than those from Omo. Some highly important discoveries have been made at Koobi Fora. Among them are femurs (thighbones) about two million years old that scientists think belong to the early form of *Homo* frequently called *habilis*. These femurs are different from *Australopithecus* femurs, suggesting that the two hominids had different leg structures.

Some anthropologists think that the Koobi Fora fossils they call *Australopithecus boisei* show a

The camp at Koobi Fora on the shores of Lake Turkana, Kenya: the many fossils found here have contributed enormously to the understanding of human evolution.

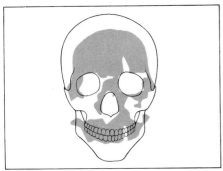

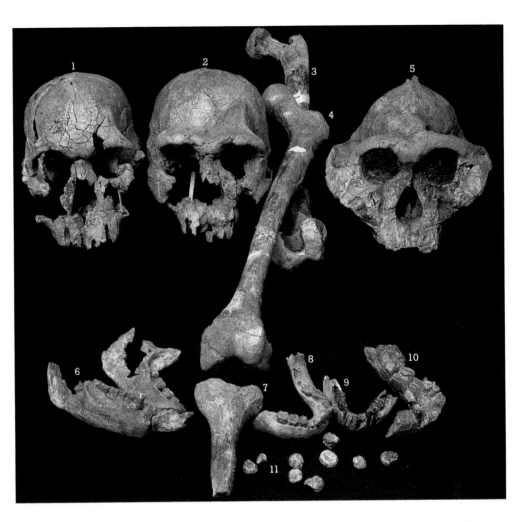

This comparison of the skull of modern man with an early Homo *skull (above and 1) shows the fossil had a smaller braincase. The early* Homo *skull is more like the* Homo erectus *skull (2) than that of* Australopithecus boisei *(5). The two femurs (3 & 4) are similar to human femurs. The tibia (7) and femur (4) show the* Homo erectus *knee joint. The jaws are from an adult* erectus *(6), an* erectus *youth (8), and an australopithecine youth (9). The hominid jaw fragment (10) is unidentified. The teeth (11) are* Australopithecus boisei. *All these fossils are from Koobi Fora.*

marked difference in size between the sexes. These scientists point out that such an extreme difference in size between the males and females has not been found in the *habilis* and *erectus* fossils from the area. In addition, a well-preserved and virtually complete skull of *Homo erectus* dated to 1.5 million years ago shows that *Homo erectus* was living at Koobi Fora at about the same time as *Australopithecus boisei*. Although the first *Homo erectus* ever discovered came from the island of Java in the 1890s, this is the oldest firmly dated *Homo erectus* fossil from Africa.

However, there is still disagreement over how many types of hominids were living at Koobi Fora. One skull – dated at between 1.7 and 1.5 million years old – has teeth that are similar to *habilis* fossils. The braincase, however, is too small to be properly called *habilis*. This find is particularly puzzling because of the discovery of yet another skull known to be older than 1.7 million years that has a very large braincase. Those who have examined both specimens are not sure what these two skulls imply. Some scientists believe that they simply show the range of individual differences within *Homo habilis*, while Richard Leakey suggests that the small-brained fossil belongs to yet another species – *Australopithecus africanus*.

These exciting finds are forcing anthropologists to ask some challenging questions: how many different hominid types were living around Koobi Fora at the same time? What might their lifestyles have been? How do the fossils found here fit into the over-all pattern of hominid evolution? For scientists involved in the study of man's origins, the answers may come from the wealth of material being excavated at Omo, Koobi Fora, Laetoli and Hadar. At present, however, there are no firm answers to these questions.

The South African Hominids

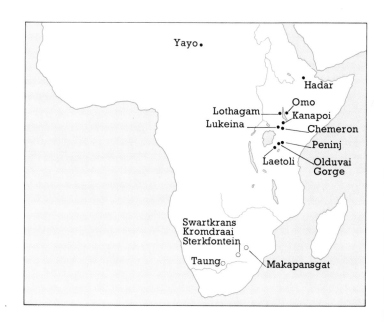

In 1924, during mining operations at Taung in Cape Province, South Africa, some fossil remains of a hominid child were discovered and sent to Raymond Dart in his capacity as professor of anatomy at the University of Witwatersrand in South Africa. The remains included an endocast of the brain, a face, and a jaw.

The importance of the Taung find was not universally recognized or accepted at the time. Most scientists in the 1920s and 1930s felt that the Taung skull was a fossil ape. This belief was supported by the conviction that the brain would be the first human feature to evolve. Scientists expected to find early human fossils with big brains and apelike teeth, but the Taung skull had a small brain and human-like teeth.

After careful study of the endocast and the face, jaw and teeth, Dart pointed out that the spinal column, which entered the skull vertically, could indicate upright walking. The small canine teeth were additional evidence that this was a hominid skull. Dart also emphasized that the dry environment at Taung would have been unsuitable for apes. He named the fossil *Australopithecus africanus*.

Later in the 1930s adult hominid fossils were discovered at other South African sites and analyzed. These hominids also had human-like teeth, but much smaller brains than those of modern humans. Gradually, the evidence was building up to support Dart's interpretation of the Taung skull. By 1959, when Louis and Mary Leakey had named their recently discovered hominid *Zinjanthropus*, the Taung skull and the stage of human evolution it represented were fully accepted by other scientists.

Most scientists today recognize two distinct species of *Australopithecus* fossils as having lived in South Africa: *Australopithecus africanus* and *Australopithecus robustus* (*robustus* = robust or heavily built). Other species are also represented by the fossils thus far recovered from the South African sites.

The Taung fossil (above) was classified as an early hominid, and named Australopithecus africanus. *It had teeth like those of a human being, but the brain was small.*

This map shows the distribution of hominid sites in Africa during the Pliocene and Early Pleistocene epochs. The open circles indicate South African cave sites. Closed circles show East African locations.

These include a very early and as yet unnamed species of the genus *Homo*. Some scientists also recognize a fourth species of hominid from these sites: *Homo erectus*.

To understand the evolutionary relationships between species, it is essential to know when they lived. This is difficult because the hominids from South Africa were all found in cave sites that lack the volcanic rocks needed for absolute dating. However, by comparing animal fossils found at the sites with similar animal fossils from such well-dated areas as the Omo site, it is possible to estimate dates for the South African hominid fossils. They probably lived at different times during the period between about 3 and 0.5 million years ago.

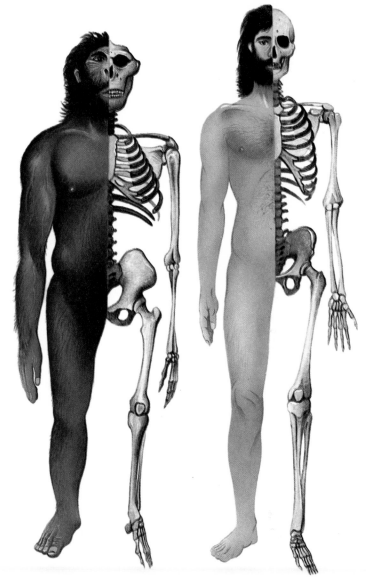

This reconstruction of Australopithecus robustus (above left) is based on fossils found in South Africa. The drawing of the human being (above right) provides a comparison with this ancient hominid.

Raymond Dart (wearing jacket) was the first to recognize that the Taung fossil was hominid. Here he discusses early African fossil hominids with Richard Leakey (far left), who has directed excavations at the East African site of Koobi Fora.

Interpreting the Evidence

Interpretations differ about the evolutionary position of the oldest hominid from South Africa, *Australopithecus africanus*, which is estimated to be two to three million years old. The fossils belonging to this species have a small brain, human-like teeth, and upright posture. Anthropologists generally agree that *Australopithecus africanus* stood about four feet in height and weighed between 65 and 90 pounds. Some scientists believe that this species has no direct connection with the evolution of modern human beings. One interpretation is that two distinct species of hominid are represented by the Hadar fossils that have been dated to between four and three million years. In this interpretation, one species has been seen as an ancestor of modern humans while the other is thought to be *Australopithecus africanus*.

Other scientists who also believe that *Australopithecus africanus* is not part of the human lineage think that *Australopithecus africanus* and modern man had a common ancestor in *Australopithecus afarensis*. To these scientists *Australopithecus africanus* is just part of a line that led to *Australopithecus robustus* and then later became extinct.

Another scientific opinion is that both *Australopithecus africanus* and *Australopithecus afarensis* represent a single species. This theory states that the species was a common ancestor of the early form of *Homo*, sometimes called *habilis* or simply early *Homo*, and of *Australopithecus robustus*, which died out.

Although there is not yet enough evidence to prove which, if any, interpretation is correct, one thing seems certain: beginning about two million years ago, there were two distinct species of hominid living in South Africa – *Australopithecus robustus* and the form called early *Homo*.

The existence of these two species was once believed to be an example of sexual dimorphism. The larger, sturdier fossils now called *Australopithecus robustus* were interpreted as males, while the more lightly built fossils now considered to be *Homo* were interpreted as females. Modern analysis has proved this theory wrong. Differences between the types of fossils indicate they had very different lifestyles.

Australopithecus robustus is estimated to have been between five and five and a half feet tall and to

The skull of Australopithecus robustus *(below right) has obvious differences when placed beside that of* Australopithecus africanus *(top right). The face appears much larger and broader in relation to the size of the braincase, and there are more pronounced ridges on the skull for the attachment of muscles.*

have weighed 110 to 155 pounds. Its distinguishing features are huge molars, with teeth-wear patterns that suggest a vegetarian diet, and a heavy facial structure that supported its massive chewing muscles. The South African fossils known as early *Homo* suggest that it was more lightly built than *Australopithecus robustus*. It had smaller molars and a larger brain. Its teeth suggest a more varied diet, including some meat, and the larger brain suggests that it was more intelligent. Most anthropologists are in agreement that this form was the ancestor of man, while *Australopithecus robustus* became extinct about one million years ago.

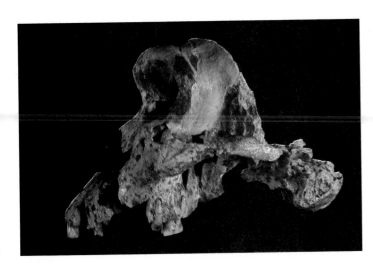

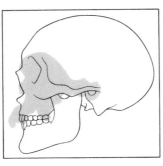

Although fragmentary, this hominid fossil (above) has rounded brow ridges, an indication that it is an early Homo. *However, the face still projects forward in comparison to that of modern man, as the diagram (right) shows.*

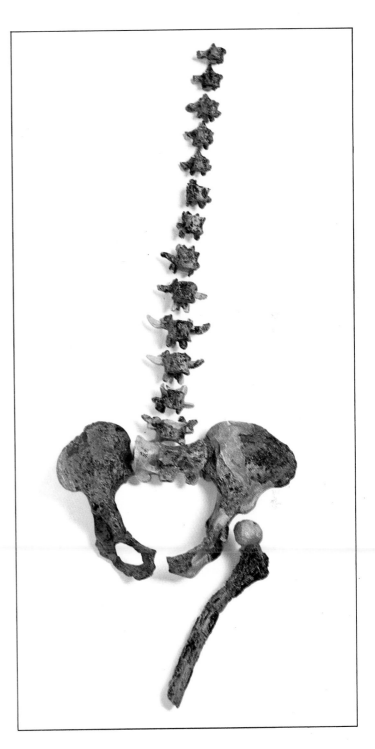

The fossilized hipbones, femur and the vertebrae of the backbone shown here were found at Sterkfontein in South Africa, and belonged to Australopithecus africanus. *The wide hipbones and the large joint where the femur fits into the hipbone indicate that this hominid walked upright.*

Life on the Savanna

Anthropologists can deduce quite a lot of information from fossil remains – for example, the possible age of the individual when it died, its size and weight, and the way it moved. On the other hand, fossils give few clues about such things as how much body hair the hominids had or what color it was. The earliest hominid fossils, in particular, tell us little about how modern man's distant ancestors lived.

The footprints found at Laetoli suggest a small group of hominids. Another group of fossils of individuals of different ages who lived slightly earlier than Lucy, and apparently died together some time between 4 million and 3.5 million years ago, have been found at Hadar. They have been called the "first family." From such fossil evidence scientists believe that man's early ancestors lived in groups in the savanna (open grassland) which then covered that part of Africa. For other information about ways in which these hominids may have lived, scientists must look at modern primates and other savanna-dwelling animals to see if any useful deductions can be made.

Living in groups appears to be a characteristic of most primates, both human and non-human. The groups usually consist of one or more adult males, several adult females, and the offspring. The size of the group depends on the type of environment, the availability of food, and the danger from predators.

There is much competition for mates between savanna-dwelling primates and only the strongest and most powerful males usually become fathers. Although the reasons are not fully understood, this type of family structure, produces a big difference in size between the males and females in a group. This is an example of sexual dimorphism – the term anthropologists give to physical differences in size between the sexes.

One of the basic differences between human and non-human primate social groups is that humans normally share all types of food. Humans also eat much more meat than do non-human primates, and food sharing is an important part of meat eating. A large animal supplies more meat than a single individual can eat. It is also easier to catch large animals if a number of individuals cooperate in hunting them together.

Some mammals that hunt in groups – social carnivores such as wild dogs, hyenas, and lions – have social groups similar in some ways to those of the early hominid families. They, too, have home bases or dens to which they return, and they share food. Humans, however, are unique in sharing not only animal food but also plant food.

In present-day human societies that live off the land and do not grow their own food, it is usually the males who hunt and the females with dependent children who collect the plant food. Each individual then shares his or her food with the rest of the group. This, too, is regarded by scientists as a clue to the way early savanna-dwelling hominids lived, although it is unlikely that fossil evidence will ever be found to show which came first: food sharing or living in groups.

These chacma baboons are savanna-living primates. Animals that live on the savanna (open grasslands) usually form large social groups, which greatly improve their chances of survival because predators are less likely to attack a group than a single animal.

This reconstruction of hominid life during the Pliocene (above) is based on fossil evidence from Africa. The hominids walked upright and ate both meat and berries. The amount and distribution of body hair, as well as skin color, is conjecture.

Social carnivores, such as lions (left), live in organized groups and cooperate when hunting. Their cubs learn hunting skills by watching the kill and sharing in the subsequent feast.

The Seed Eaters

For many years the evolution of those features unique to man – brain size and intelligence, bipedal walking and the hominid teeth and jaw shapes – were linked to tool use. The theory went like this: some primates use their large, dagger-like canine teeth to defend themselves. Once primates started using and carrying tools and weapons, the weapons fulfilled the same function as the canines, which, because they no longer needed to be so large and strong, evolved into smaller hominid canines.

There is a major problem with this theory. Some fossil evidence suggests that the reduction in the size of the canine teeth, as well as the development of other human dental features, was under way approximately 16 million years ago. The first good archaeological evidence for tool use dates to only a little over two million years ago. The cause therefore seems to appear 14 million years after the effect!

In 1970 the British anthropologist Clifford Jolly put forward another explanation for the reduction in size of the canine teeth. He based his theory on the diet, teeth, and jaws of present-day and fossil gelada

A male gelada baboon reveals its teeth as it rolls back its upper lip. Although it looks so fierce, its diet consists of plant material, such as stems and roots.

The tough grasses and roots that form the diet of the gelada (right) have resulted in a flatter, deeper face, larger back teeth, and shorter canines than in the long-faced baboon (far right), which eats more tender grasses and fruit. Although the differences are slight, they are sufficient to show how features can alter among closely-related groups when they have different diets.

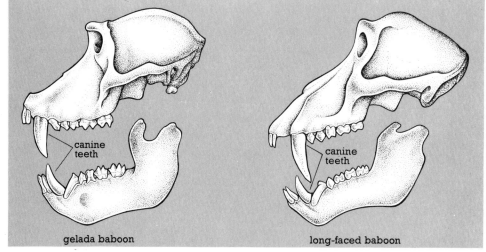

gelada baboon

long-faced baboon

The grass cover of a typical savanna, for example the Serengeti Plain of Tanzania (above), is open grassland interspersed with bushes and trees. A diet of small, tough foodstuffs, such as seeds, is readily available in this environment. Some scientists consider that the explanation for such features in early hominids as the shortened face and small canine teeth lies in their adaptation to the harsh foods typical of the savanna.

baboons. Geladas live in the highlands of Ethiopia, a dry environment, where they feed on foodstuffs such as grasses, stems and roots, a much harsher diet than that of other baboons. Compared with other baboons, geladas' faces are slightly flatter, their jaws a little deeper, and their canines and their incisors (front teeth) are fractionally smaller.

The same comparison can be made between apes and hominids, although the ape-hominid contrast is much greater. This comparison suggests that diet may have been the cause of the evolution of human dental and facial characteristics. The flat face and heavy jaws of the early hominids, with the associated change in position of the chewing muscles, would increase the chewing force of the molars. Small

hominid canine teeth would allow the jaws to move from side to side, not just up and down, and the molars could then work as millstones to crush and grind the tough foodstuffs found on the savanna.

There are, nonetheless, differences in structure between gelada teeth and human teeth. Human molars are flatter than gelada molars, and the enamel on human teeth is thicker. These differences suggest that the early humans had a different diet from the geladas: possibly their first important source of food was seeds. The flat hominid molars could crush and grind hard-shelled seeds and were protected from this tough chewing by their especially thick enamel. The seed-eating hypothesis, as this idea is called, suggests that the earliest human ancestors began to eat seeds when they moved from the forests into the savanna, and that this change was an early step in human evolution.

The seed-eating theory is important because it suggests that diet and not tool use was responsible for the evolution of human-like teeth. However, it is based primarily on the comparative anatomy of modern primates, and not on fossils. Before the theory can be accepted it must be tested against the evidence from the fossils of man's earliest Miocene ancestors.

Using Tools

The development of the manufacture and use of tools by man's early ancestors is a highly important step on the pathway of human evolution. The earliest recognizable tools are stone tools that have been termed "Oldowan" after Olduvai Gorge where they were first discovered. Today Oldowan tools are also known from a number of other African sites. The earliest evidence of such tools comes from Hadar, Ethiopia, in deposits that are about 2.5 million years old.

Oldowan tools are either crudely modified pebbles or flakes struck from pebbles. The pebbles themselves are roughly flaked on both sides of an edge and are called core tools. They were probably used for chopping and hacking. Flakes that have been modified for finer cutting and scraping are termed flake tools.

Oldowan tools are often found at hominid campsites together with animal bones, or at kill- or butchering-sites. Although this suggests that the tools were used for butchering, they may have also been used for gathering and preparing plant food.

In the oldest fossil bed at Olduvai, about 1.9 million years old, there is a large area with tools and the remains of many different types of animals – perhaps a campsite to which the hominids brought back meat they had scavenged or killed elsewhere. Also at this site is a rough circle of stones, measuring thirteen to sixteen feet in diameter. This could have formed the foundation for a structure of branches to make a hut of windbreak, and its construction might have involved using tools. In all, there are ten known living-sites and two kill- or butchering-sites at Olduvai.

Approximately two million years ago, therefore, some of man's early ancestors were making and using stone tools and possibly also building shelters. The early toolmakers at Olduvai could have been *Homo habilis* or *Australopithecus boisei*, or perhaps even both. A number of factors suggest that *Homo habilis* was the more prolific toolmaker. For example, the dental and facial proportions of *Homo habilis* show it was an omnivore – it had a mixed diet which included meat. Because many of the stone tools are associated with butchered animals, *Homo habilis* probably made them. In contrast, the teeth and jaws of *Australo-*

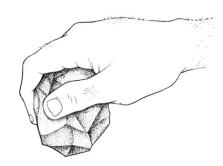

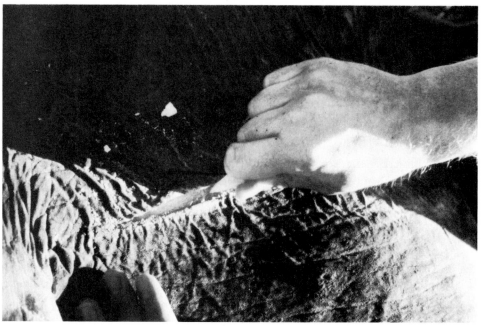

The diagram above and the photograph right show how man's hominid ancestors probably held and used stone tools. In the photograph a modern copy of a flake tool is used to cut elephant hide – showing just how efficient these tools could be.

A group of Homo habilis *makes and uses stone tools at their campsite. In the background of this artist's impressions is a hut. A large circle of stones, perhaps the remains of a hut like this, was found at Olduvai.*

Two large teardrop-shaped hand axes and two animal bones, lying as they were found at Olorgesailie in Kenya, a site excavated by Louis and Mary Leakey from 1943 to 1947 and dating to about 400,000 years ago. Perhaps the axes were used to kill and cut up the animals to which the bones belonged.

pithecus boisei show it was vegetarian. Furthermore, *Homo habilis* had a larger brain than *Australopithecus boisei*. This suggests that *Homo habilis* had a more complicated lifestyle which could have included developing skills as a tool user and toolmaker.

Although the first evidence of tools in the fossil record are Oldowan stone tools, it is likely that hominids living more than 2.5 million years ago first made and used tools of perishable materials, such as wood or skin, that did not become fossilized. Present-day chimpanzees use simple tools – twigs to prod for termites in termite mounds, and leaf sponges to soak up otherwise inaccessible water. Early hominids may have used tools in this fashion. Also, if food sharing was indeed an early part of the human lifestyle, bags of animal skin or portable bowls of wood or bark would have been necessary to carry plant food to the home-base or campsite. However, because such materials do not fossilize, it is unlikely that any evidence of them will ever be found.

Evolution of the Human Brain

Human intelligence includes not only the ability to think but also the ability to speak. The hominids of the Pliocene and the Early Pleistocene are known to have been like present-day man in the general pattern of their teeth and in the way they walked. But how similar were they to man in their intellectual abilities? The answer lies in the brain – in particular its size, its organization and the proportions of its various parts.

While there are no fossilized brains, scientists can tell a great deal about the brains of hominids from the impressions left on the inside of the cranial cavity, the part of the skull that houses the brain. Occasionally, natural casts of the inside of the skull are found. These casts show the relative size and shape of the major regions of the cerebral cortex, the outer layer of the brain.

In the great apes of today, the occipital lobe which is concerned with vision is large. The temporal lobe which controls memory and the parietal lobe, which governs the senses of touch and general body awareness, are relatively small. In man the reverse is true. All the hominids from the Pliocene and the Early Pleistocene have the distinct human pattern. These hominids include *Australopithecus africanus*, which may have lived as long ago as three and a half million years, and the vegetarians *Australopithecus robustus* and *Australopithecus boisei*, as well as the tool-using early members of the genus *Homo*.

Why do these hominids, so different in their life-styles, all have brains that appear distinctly human? One recent theory suggests that brain development could be related to bipedal walking. The physical and mental coordination necessary to move on two legs would be reflected in increased growth of the parietal region that controls these activities.

The reason is probably not as straightforward as this. All these hominids were living in open country, more exposed to predators than in the forest. To

In this comparison of the brain sizes and body weights of hominids and apes, increases are shown, for simplicity, as straight lines. The steep rise of the line to man from his ancestors shows that, as Homo *evolved and grew heavier, brain size increased more rapidly than would be accounted for by greater body weight. The gentle rise of the lines for apes and australopithecines shows that their larger brains only kept pace with increases in body weight.*

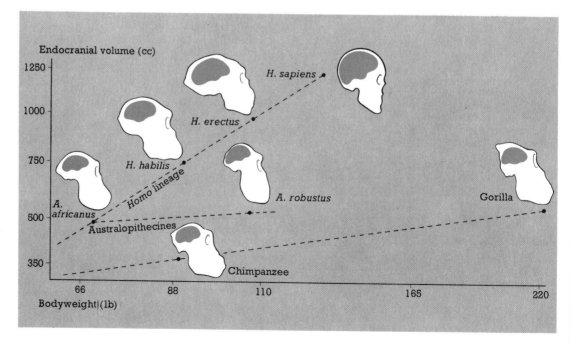

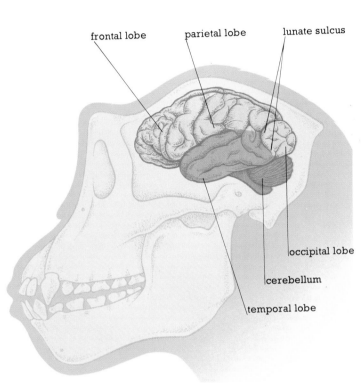

frontal lobe   parietal lobe   lunate sulcus

occipital lobe

cerebellum

temporal lobe

chimpanzee

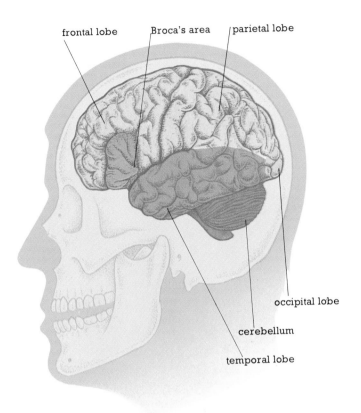

frontal lobe   Broca's area   parietal lobe

occipital lobe

cerebellum

temporal lobe

human

survive it is likely that they would have required more sophisticated sight, hearing, sense of smell, and social behavior – for instance, the ability to communicate quickly with each other. In fact the area in the human brain concerned with language is also large and convoluted in fossils of these early hominids. Does this mean that these hominids could speak? Unfortunately there is not enough evidence to be sure.

Endocranial measurements can, however, show the total brain size of the hominids. The brains of humans are much larger than the brains of other living primates. When body size is taken into account, the australopithecines had brains slightly larger than those of apes, while the brains of *Homo habilis* and *Homo erectus* are still larger. Although scientists are not at all sure why this happened, it is a fact that the human brain has slowly increased in size throughout the thousands of centuries over which man's evolution has taken place.

The differences between the brain of a chimpanzee (left) and that of a human (right) are shown in these two diagrams. The skulls are shown in pale yellow and the orange background areas represent the complete face. The functions of the areas of the brain are similar in all primates: the cerebellum controls muscular coordination, the occipital lobe handles vision, the frontal lobe deals with movement, the parietal lobe is concerned with sensory information, and the temporal lobe is concerned with memory. The lunate sulcus that separates the occipital from the parietal region is not prominent in humans. Fossil hominids, unlike the apes, share the human pattern of brain proportions: large temporal and parietal lobes, a relatively small occipital lobe and an expanded speech center called Broca's area, which is completely lacking in the apes.

The Hairless Ape

Human beings are unique among their primate relatives in being comparatively hairless. Did man's ancestors once have considerable body hair? If so, when did they lose it? There can be no answer from the fossil record, but scientists have put forward suggestions, basing their theories on the function of hairlessness.

Humans perspire much more than any other animal except the rhesus monkey. For the hairless human, evaporation of perspiration is a highly efficient way of cooling the body, particularly when the humidity is low. The savanna of Africa, the homeland of early human ancestors, is hot and low in humidity. Because of this scientists suggested that lack of hair and body cooling by evaporation first evolved when man's ancestors began to live in hot open country.

This theory has a major weakness: no other animals in this type of environment cool themselves by the combination of hairlessness and high sweat production. On the contrary many savanna animals have dense hair or fur that reflects much of the heat and also provides an insulating air space to protect the skin from the heat which is not reflected. Humans have retained thick hair only on their heads, the part of the body exposed to direct sun in bipedal walking. This head hair helps to insulate the human brain, which is sensitive to overheating.

Another argument against this theory is that studies of modern humans show that the combination of hairlessness and high sweat production is not the most efficient means of avoiding overheating in hot, savanna-like conditions. Modern humans wearing light clothing roughly equivalent in insulation to body hair remain cooler and perspire less in similar hot, dry conditions than nude humans unaccustomed to such conditions.

This research suggests that human ancestors became hairless while living in forests and before they began living in the open country. There is no clear reason why hair loss should have occurred in the forest, but there are some clues. In tropical forests the humidity is higher, the air stiller, and the temperature lower than on the savanna. In these conditions,

Orangutans have relatively sparse body hair compared with many other primates. The typical almost hairless patches, clearly visible on this female with her baby, may help increase heat loss through radiation.

The Tasady people live in the remote tropical forests of the Philippine Islands of southeast Asia. Some scientists believe that early ancestors of man began to lose their body hair when they lived in forests such as these because in such a humid environment it was more efficient to lose body heat through radiating it rather than through the evaporation of perspiration.

Desert peoples, such as these Moroccan sheep farmers (left), wear long, loose robes as insulation against the sun's rays and the hot climate in which they live. Air movement beneath the robes circulates heat away from the skin.

particularly where humidity is high, cooling by evaporation would be inefficient. Most forest animals cool themselves by radiating their body heat through the skin.

Less dense hair on the body would probably assist the radiation of heat in large-bodied forest animals with relatively great areas of skin. One of the largest living primates, the orangutan of the tropical forests of Borneo and Sumatra, has not only very sparse hair but also large, almost naked patches on its stomach, chest, and thighs. Although much more evidence is needed, it seems likely that man's early ancestors started to lose their body hair while in the forest, and were well on their way to hairlessness when they first entered the savanna.

African Origins

The African fossil sites provide the earliest record of man's ancestors. There is a recognizable pattern of progress from the oldest evidence so far discovered of bipedal hominids at Laetoli and Hadar through the South African *Australopithecus africanus* to the appearance of the genus *Homo*, and to the larger robust vegetarian australopithecines. The details of that progress, however, and the exact relationship of the different fossil remains both to each other and to man are not so easy to establish with certainty.

The significance of the oldest hominid fossils from Africa is particularly difficult to assess because there are few of them and some are very fragmentary, and finally because anthropologists are not – as so often happens – in agreement about which fossils ought to be included in the hominid classification. They do agree that the australopithecines and *Homo* had a common ancestor. They disagree, however, about when the australopithecine and *Homo* lines split and started to develop separately, about who the common ancestor might be, and even about which fossils are called *Homo* and which *Australopithecus*.

If early *Homo* extended back to or beyond the time of Hadar and Laetoli (about four million years), as Richard and Mary Leakey suggest, the split between early *Homo* and the line leading to *Australopithecus robustus* and *Australopithecus boisei* would be older than four million years ago. However, an alternative interpretation of the Hadar and Laetoli material suggested by Don Johanson, the excavator of Hadar, would put the split at three million years ago. Some other anthropologists believe that *Australopithecus africanus*, as represented by the South African specimens of that name, is the same type of hominid as the older fossils from Hadar and Laetoli. In this view the split could be as recent as two million years ago.

There is somewhat less controversy as the fossils become younger. Most anthropologists place the early *Homo* form originally classified as *Homo habilis* from Olduvai Gorge, on the direct line of human evolution to *Homo erectus* and so on to modern man. However, other fossils that have been dated at about the same age as the Olduvai *habilis* specimens have become controversial. The majority of fossils from this time are not well preserved. They are often missing critical parts used in the classification process – such as teeth or braincase. In addition, whatever the fragments themselves suggest, they can not be viewed in isolation. Conclusions about them can not be reached until the *habilis* specimens are taken into account.

Despite all the searching, speculation and controversy over individual fossils, there seems to be general agreement, based on the fossil evidence, that hominids did develop in Africa.

The reasons for the African development, however, are not completely understood. The discovery of more fossils and continuing analysis of the environmental conditions in Africa between four million and one million years ago may provide some of the answers. There seems, however, little doubt that the development of such distinctly human features as food sharing, tool use and home bases occurred in Africa during this three million year period. It was characteristics such as these that enabled man's ancestors to move to and survive in the colder and drier areas in Europe and Asia.

The diagram (opposite) shows how two anthropologists, Don Johanson (left) and Richard Leakey (right), think the hominid species evolved. Johanson believes the fossils he named Australopithecus afarensis *are the common ancestor of* Homo *and* Australopithecus africanus *and* Australopithecus robustus. *He also considers that* Australopithecus boisei *is the same as* Australopithecus robustus. *Richard Leakey, whose views have changed as the fossil record has increased, currently sees all the* Australopithecus *specimens as a sidebranch of hominid evolution. He does not accept* afarensis *as a separate species. The status of* Ramapithecus *is controversial and neither Johanson nor Leakey regard it as an ancestor. Leakey, however, sees* Ramapithecus *as another sidebranch in evolution which became extinct about two million years ago.*

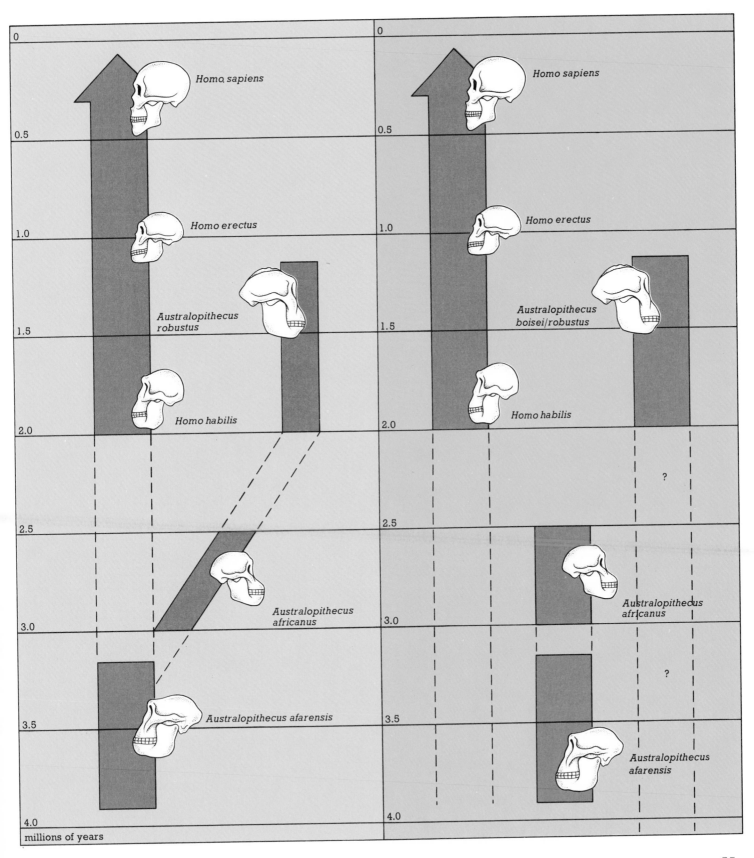

millions of years

The Fossils from Java

In the early 1890s the first fossils of *Homo erectus* were found on the tropical island of Java, now part of Indonesia, by a Dutch scientist and army doctor, Eugène Dubois. The fossils found by him are known popularly as Java Man, although later discoveries showed that *Homo erectus* has also lived elsewhere and probably did not originate in Java.

In 1890 Dubois went to Trinil on the Solo River, where in the next two years he found a tooth, part of a skull and a femur. The femur looked like that of a human being who walked upright, while the skull was small and primitive, with thick bone and long, low contours. This was a surprise to Dubois and other scientists of this time, because they expected to find hominid fossils with large, human-like brains and skulls, together with apelike bodies. Java Man, however, had the opposite characteristics and many scientists refused to accept these fossils as true human ancestors.

In 1894 Dubois named these fossils *Pithecanthropus erectus* (*Pithecanthropus* = ape man, *erectus* after the femur that indicated upright walking). This name has since been changed to *Homo erectus* to emphasize the close evolutionary relationship of this type of early hominid to modern *Homo sapiens*.

Although Dubois never returned to Java after 1896, work was resumed in the 1930s, when the German paleontologist G. H. R. von Koenigswald renewed Dubois' excavations. He concentrated his work at the site called Sangiran that had deposits not only of the same age as Dubois' fossils but also older.

Absolute dating has shown that the deposits from which Dubois' fossils came were between about 800,000 and 500,000 years old. The earlier beds that von Koenigswald worked on may be as old as 1.9 million years, the same age as the oldest bed at Olduvai and the date of the first generally accepted appearance of the genus *Homo* in the African sites. Indonesian scientists resumed the work at the site

These three fossil fragments of skulls and part of an upper jaw (bottom) are fossils of Homo erectus *discovered by G. H. R. von Koenigswald in the late 1930s. The fossil at top right is from the remains that are known informally as* Pithecanthropus II. *(*Pithecanthropus *was the first scientific name for hominids from Java.) The other fossils are from* Pithecanthropus IV, *and date to about 1.9 million years ago.*

after World War II. Fossils representing more than thirty individuals of *Homo erectus* have now been recovered.

The classification of von Koeingswald's most interesting fossils, found in deposits at Sangiran known as the Djetis beds, is disputed by scientists. Some believe that they could be an Asian type of *Australopithecus*; other scientists regard them as most similar to the more advanced *Homo habilis* from Africa. However, most scientists agree that the fossils belonged to hominids who migrated from Africa across India to southeast Asia before two million years ago. However, there is no direct fossil evidence for this migration nor any indication of precisely when it might have taken place. Indeed, some scientists, such as von Koenigswald himself, suggest that human evolution took place throughout Africa and Asia, and that the known fossils from Africa and Java represent the extreme geographical ranges of hominids at this time. This may be true since scientists cannot be sure that, just because the earliest human fossils come from Africa, this was the only area in which early human evolution was occurring.

The Homo erectus *femur from Java (below left) is very like a modern femur (below right). This suggests that* Homo erectus *moved in the same way as modern man.*

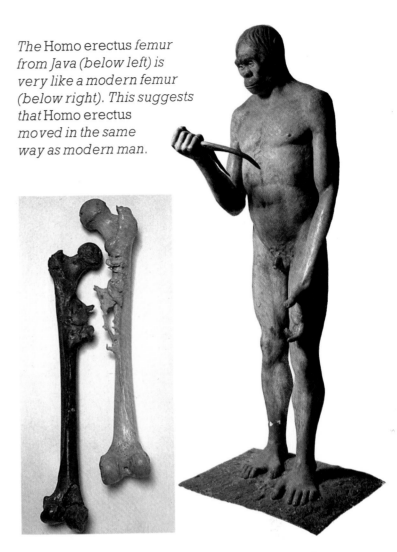

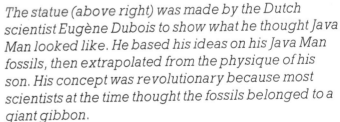

The statue (above right) was made by the Dutch scientist Eugène Dubois to show what he thought Java Man looked like. He based his ideas on his Java Man fossils, then extrapolated from the physique of his son. His concept was revolutionary because most scientists at the time thought the fossils belonged to a giant gibbon.

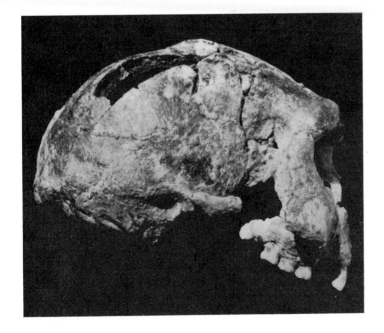

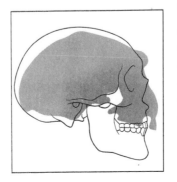

The fossil Homo erectus *skull (far left), found at Sangiran, Java, in the 1960s, has an almost intact face. Superimposing it on an outline of a modern human skull (left) shows that the facial bones were more massive than modern man's.*

Peking Man

A molar tooth that could possibly have been hominid was found in a Chinese drugstore in 1899. Traditional Chinese drugstores, now as then, are not unusual places to make fossil discoveries, because for centuries the Chinese have ground up fossil teeth to use as medicines. At the time it aroused a good deal of interest among paleontologists and anthropologists although it is now thought to be an ape's tooth.

In the 1920s expeditions from both Sweden and the United States went to China to search for evidence of early man. The Swedish expedition succeeded in finding two hominid teeth at a site called Choukou-tien – "Dragon Bone Hill" – a site rich in fossils near Peking. These hominid teeth excited the attention of Davidson Black, a Canadian doctor teaching in Peking. Eager to find more fossils of early man, Black started working at the Choukoutien excavations and in the late 1920s found a third hominid tooth there.

Black classified the hominid teeth as belonging to a new species – *Sinanthropus pekinensis* (*Sin* = China, *anthropus* = human being, *pekinensis* = Peking). It is now more usually called Peking Man. Many scientists at the time thought Black unwise in trying to establish a new fossil species from a few teeth. However, subsequent excavations at Choukoutien uncovered fossils of over forty hominds – both adults and children – as well as remains of stone tools, evidence of the use of fire, and plant and animal foods. In recent years, these fossils of Peking Man, like those of Java Man, have been classified as belonging to the species *Homo erectus*. They represent the richest collection of *Homo erectus* fossils from any single small area in the world.

Unfortunately most of these fossils were lost during

This artist's impression of a Homo erectus *family in their cave home at Choukoutien, China, is based on work done by scientists at the site. On the left, one of the family skins a dead animal. Beside the fire another makes a stone tool. The female brings in some plant food, while the youngest member of the family picks up the head of a newly killed deer.*

World War II. Just before the Japanese captured Peking in 1941, these valuable fossils were packed up to be shipped to the United States for safekeeping. They disappeared between Peking and the port of Chinhuangtao. During the 1970s tremendous efforts were made to trace the fossils, but without success.

The fossils, however, are not completely lost to the scientific world. After Black's death in 1934, the German scientist Franz Weidenreich prepared excellent drawings, casts, and descriptions of the fossils that today provide information about them. In addition, in the 1960s the Chinese resumed excavations at the site, and have recovered new fossils of Peking Man.

The age of Peking Man is difficult to determine. However, Chinese scientists have recently applied absolute dating techniques to the Choukoutien deposits. Combined with the animal remains found in the cave these datings suggest that Peking Man occupied the cave some time between 600,000 and 200,000 years ago.

The Middle Pleistocene temperature at Choukoutien was warm and hospitable in the summer, but cold in the winter. In order to survive the cold, Peking Man used fire. There are four areas of ash concentration in the Choukoutien cave, and one is an amazing twenty feet deep, showing that fire burned in this area for a very long time.

Although Peking Man used fire, it is not known if he could make it. Nor is it known whether he wore animal skins, although this seems likely because of the cold winters. But through ingenuity and intelligence, *Homo erectus* was certainly able to live successfully in an environment that would have been unsuitable for earlier human ancestors. Thus *Homo erectus* is truly an early human rather than an apeman.

The cave at Choukoutien (above) where a large number of fossils representing Peking Man were found. In places the deposits at this site are a remarkable 130 feet deep.

 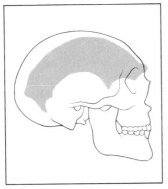

Because the original fossils of Peking Man were lost, scientists work from casts. The skull cap (far left) is a cast of one of the original fossils found at Choukoutien. The diagram (left) shows the skull in gray superimposed on an outline of a modern human skull.

The Ice Ages

The geological epoch known as the Pleistocene spanned the period between 1.75 million years ago and about 10,000 years ago – the time of the Ice Ages. Although there were hominids in the Pliocene, and perhaps even, with the apelike *Ramapithecus*, in the Miocene, it was during the Pleistocene that the marked expansion of the human brain, sophisticated tool use, and the spread of hominids throughout the world all occured.

The Pleistocene was an extraordinary period in terms of climate: a succession of very cold periods were interspersed by warm spells. Periodically throughout the Pleistocene, sheets of ice spread out from the polar regions, covering large areas of the Americas, Europe, and northern Asia. During these periods the mean annual temperature in the northern latitudes was much lower, perhaps more than 20°F, than it is today.

In some areas south of the ice sheets in Asia, North America, and Europe, there may have been as few as forty or fifty frost-free days in the year. Some of the ice sheets covered as much as twenty million square miles and measured 7000 feet thick. The last major ice advance may have been under way about

During the Ice Ages some of the unglaciated areas of the world, particularly in the northern hemisphere, would have been comparable to the modern tundra landscape of Norway, shown below.

The dense woodland in this picture grows on the slopes of the African Rift valley in Kenya. Scientists believe that woodlands and forests like this spread over much of Africa during the Ice Ages.

This frigid, glaciated landscape in present-day Greenland duplicates the extreme climatic conditions at the time of the Pleistocene when much of the northern hemisphere was covered by ice.

100,000 years ago and lasted until about 10,000 years ago, the date that marks not only the end of this ice advance but also what many scientists regard as the end of the Pleistocene epoch.

The change in climate produced by these ice advances had a marked effect on human evolution and the development of human culture, especially in the northern parts of the world, which hominids had already begun to occupy. In these regions not only was the temperature low, but also major changes were taking place in the unglaciated landscape. The forests, woodlands, and grasslands of the warmer periods gave way to frozen tundra (a treeless expanse with a permanently frozen subsoil) in much of the northern hemisphere.

The climate in Africa was not affected as dramatically as the climate of the northern hemisphere during the Pleistocene. Africa was not covered by large continental ice sheets, although there were major changes in the vegetation. Montane forests of tall, hardwood trees spread across the whole continent, lowland forests of typical jungle growth almost disappeared, and deserts expanded.

During each glacial period a large quantity of water was locked up in the ice on land. This lowered the sea level, sometimes as much as four hundred feet. Where the ocean was shallow, this lower sea level exposed land that connected islands or continents. Around 1.9 million years ago, long before the invention of boats, there may have been hominids in Java who simply walked there from the Eurasian landmass. Although there is still much to learn about the relationship between man's evolution and the extreme climatic changes in this epoch, the Pleistocene certainly had a great effect on man's biological evolution and the evolution of his intelligence.

Biological evolution is a slow process. Modern humans have the ability to adapt much faster to changing environmental conditions through intelligence than through biological evolution. The use of fire, and the creation of clothing to protect the body against cold, as well as different techniques for hunting and making increasingly elaborate tools are all examples of behavioral development resulting from growing intelligence. The gradual enlargement in brain size throughout this period probably reflects an increasing reliance on intelligence as an adaptive strategy.

Fire

Fire was the first natural force that hominids learned to control and put to their own use. This was a significant step in man's evolutionary journey, helping to further separate human beings from their non-human animal relatives.

The earliest well-documented evidence of the use of fire by hominids comes from early in the Pleistocene. In Kenya burned clay has been found at the site of Chesowanja, together with stone tools and animal fossils. This site has been accurately dated to 1.4 million years ago. It is unlikely that the burned clay at this site was produced by a brush fire, because natural fires rarely reach a sufficiently high temperature for long enough to bake the ground, while controlled camp fires often do.

Although no hominid fossils were found with the burned clay at Chesowanja, it is likely, because of the site's age, that *Homo erectus* was responsible for this first evidence of a hominid using fire.

Early evidence for the use of fire has also been found in China. Archaeologists have reported ashes at the site of Yuanmou in Yunnan Province in the same earth strata as two front teeth. These teeth belonged to an early *Homo erectus* that certainly lived more than one million years ago. Charred bones, antlers and horses' teeth have been recovered from another Chinese site, Xihoudu in southern Shensi Province. Although no human fossils have been found at this site, stone tools were found, together with the burned remains of animal bone. This suggests that *Homo erectus* was making these tools, and perhaps cooking food, at least one million years ago.

Some scientists doubt that *Homo erectus* was responsible for the ashes and burned bones at the Yuanmou and Xihoudu sites. But there is no doubt that he used fire at the large cave in Choukoutien. The thickest layer of ashes there is twenty feet deep, while a second layer along the wall of the cave is thirteen feet deep in some places. Many of the bones and tools of Peking Man were found around the edge of this layer. The depth of the ashes and their concentration in the deposits suggest that *Homo erectus* could control fire. The mass of bones and tools around

Rock- and spear-wielding hunters close in on elephants for the kill — an artist's impression of how big game was caught at Torralba in Spain by Homo erectus *about 400,000 years ago. At this site (also shown opposite) the bones of many animals, together with traces of fire, were found in and around the remains of an ancient swamp. This suggests that the hunters deliberately set fire to the surrounding bush to drive animals into the marshy ground. There the animals became trapped and so were easier to kill.*

the ashes indicates that fire was the focus of life in the cave.

The earliest evidence for the use of fire in Europe comes from the Escale cave near Marseilles in France. There, traces of charcoal and ashes, fire-cracked stones, and fire-reddened hearth areas suggest that hominids were using fire about 750,000 years ago, although not all scientists accept this.

There is, however, definite evidence of man-controlled fire in other European sites later in the Middle Pleistocene. At Vértesszöllös in Hungary, a large number of burned bones was found in the same deposits as a large *Homo erectus*-like occipital bone (a bone from the back of the head) that is about 400,000 years old.

Like all primates, humans were originally and basically tropical animals. Fire, which provided warmth, was undoubtedly important when they moved into cooler northern regions. However, the earliest evidence of man-controlled fire suggests that its original use may have been for something else – perhaps the cooking of animal food. Fire also could have aided hunting and a camp fire at night would have ensured the safety of the hominids from predators.

Scientists carefully sift the earth for fossils at Torralba, Spain, where a modern iron pipe (foreground) had already been laid through the site, making the researchers' work more difficult than usual. At this location, which scientists believe was a hunting site, the remains of 30 elephants, 25 horses, 25 deer, 10 wild oxen and 6 rhinoceroses have been found.

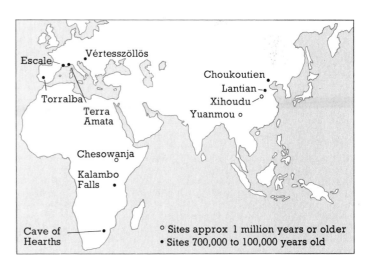

Sites that show early evidence of the use of fire. The earliest African site, Chesowanja in Kenya, may be as old as 1.4 million years. Chinese experts think Yuanmou's ash and burned bones could be as old as 1.7 million years.

Where *Homo erectus* Lived

Fossil remains from Africa and Asia show that *Homo erectus* lived over a very wide area. The best-known examples of *Homo erectus* come from Java, Choukoutien in China, and from East Africa. However, other *Homo erectus* fossils have been found in Asia and Africa, and more may yet be discovered.

In 1965 a skull, part of the face, and a jaw of *Homo erectus* were discovered in China, at Lantian in Shensi Province. The skull of Lantian Man, as these fossils are known, has a very flat forehead behind large brow ridges. Study of the animals found with Lantian Man suggests that these fossils are probably about 800,000 and 500,000 years old.

There is a collection of eleven skulls from Java that are younger than Trinil but older than 100,000 years. Known collectively as Solo Man, these skulls resemble *Homo erectus*, although they have larger braincases than the earlier Java Man.

Homo erectus fossils found in North Africa come from Ternifine in Algeria and are close to 500,000 years old. They comprise three jaws, part of a bone from the side of the skull, and a few teeth.

Although some of the hominid fossils found in France and Germany were once considered to be examples of *Homo erectus*, anthropologists are now reexamining these classifications. However, the stone tools thought to have been used by *Homo erectus* were first identified in St. Acheul, France. The tool culture associated with *erectus* – known as Acheulian after the French site – appeared about 1.2 million years ago in Africa. It is also found elsewhere in Europe, western Asia, and India.

One of the culture's characteristic tools is a teardrop-shaped stone hand ax, flaked or sharpened on both surfaces to give a good cutting edge. This ax was probably used for butchering and plant-gathering. Other types of tools characteristic of the Acheulian culture are cleavers, scrapers, and small flakes

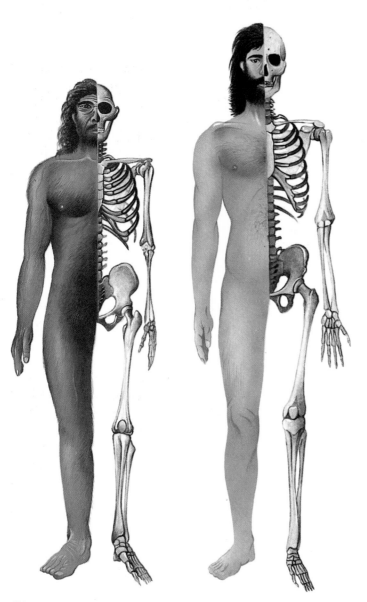

A reconstruction of what Homo erectus *(left) probably looked like. All the fossil evidence suggests he was shorter than modern* Homo sapiens, *but otherwise very similar.*

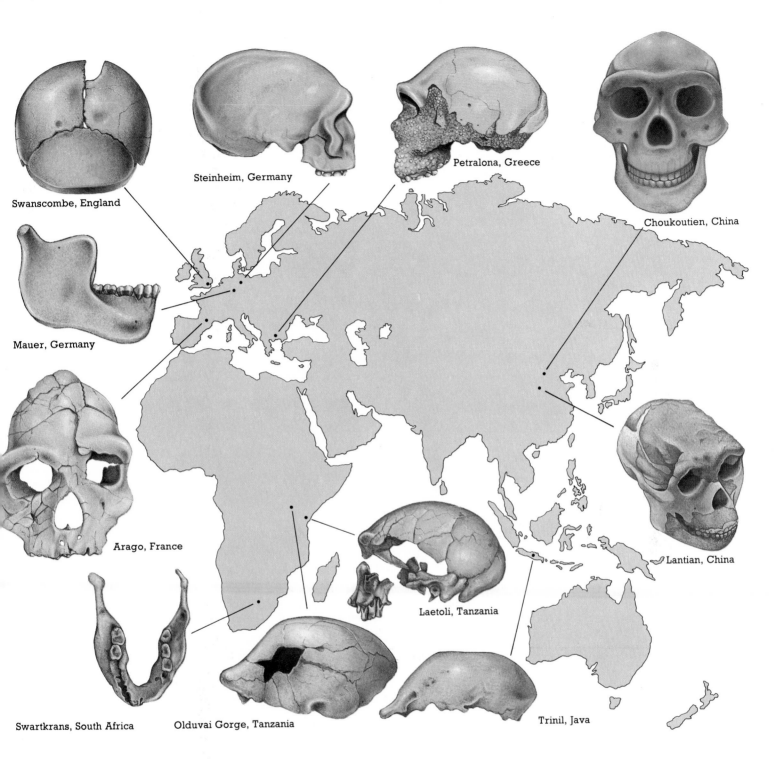

Swanscombe, England

Steinheim, Germany

Petralona, Greece

Choukoutien, China

Mauer, Germany

Arago, France

Lantian, China

Swartkrans, South Africa

Olduvai Gorge, Tanzania

Laetoli, Tanzania

Trinil, Java

which were most likely used for skinning and butchering animals. The tools of *Homo erectus* are generally more specialized and more finely made than are the tools of earlier hominids. In fact they were made, almost unchanged, by *Homo sapiens* in Europe and Africa up to 100,000 years ago, which shows how effective they must have been.

Fossils definitely identified as Homo erectus *have been found at Olduvai, Swartkrans, Java, Lantian and Choukoutien. The European sites and Laetoli indicated on the map are more controversial. Fossils from these sites have some characteristics common to* erectus, *but other features are thought to be more properly termed* Homo sapiens.

European Fossils

No one knows exactly when hominids first began to live in Europe. Recently studied sites throughout Europe contain stone tools that may be well over a million years old. If the age of these sites is correct, hominids were living in Europe long before Peking Man existed in China. Unfortunately, there are no fossils at these sites to indicate what the hominids looked like.

However, beginning with Heidelberg Man, the name given to the fossil found in 1907 at Mauer, near Heidelberg, West Germany, there is a scattering of hominid fossils and a large number of stone tools that may be as old as 500,000 years. The fossils suggest that these inhabitants of Europe were large. The Heidelberg jaw is as big as the biggest *Homo erectus* jaws from Asia and Africa. It was originally thought to be around 700,000 years old and considered an example of *Homo erectus*. Recent studies suggest that it is between 500,000 and 350,000 years old and that it has some *sapiens* as well as *erectus* features. For this reason, many anthropologists consider it a transition between the two.

There is a complete skull from the cave of Petralona in northern Greece, which may be anywhere from more than 400,000 to 200,000 years old. This controversial skull has a thick cranium which makes it look like *erectus*. Other features are like *sapiens*. The skull is in good condition and has been examined by many scientists. In one study, the British paleontologist Christopher Stringer analyzed 21 key features. The Petralona skull has six like *erectus*, eight in the *sapiens* range, and seven in between. Doctor Stringer concluded that the skull is a primitive form of *sapiens* which he calls archaic *Homo sapiens*.

There are teeth and a large occipital bone from Vértesszöllös in Hungary, and several skull fragments and a tooth from Bilzingsleben in West Germany. Fossils from Arago in south-western France include jaws and a nearly complete face, as well as skull

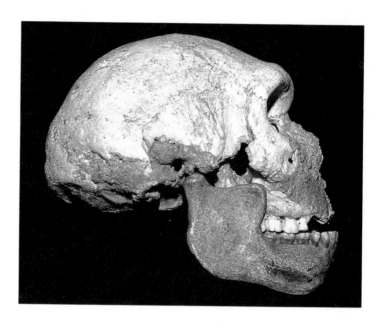

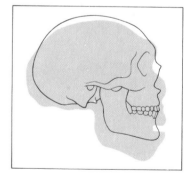

The fossil Heidelberg jaw is shown above with the skull from Petralona, Greece. Their fit is not anatomically correct. The diagram (right) compares the Petralona skull (in gray) with a modern human one (in black).

pieces and individual teeth. Although the age of these sites is uncertain – Arago and Bilzingsleben could be older than 200,000. The fossils all suggest a large hominid.

In 1933 a nearly complete skull was recovered from Steinheim in West Germany. Although the brow ridges are large, this skull is smaller than Petralona and Arago. The face is flatter than that of the Petralona skull, and the part of the skull housing the brain is

The cave at Petralona in which the well preserved skull illustrated opposite was found. The cave is in limestone hills; the beautiful rock shapes are stalactites and stalagmites, icicle-like formations often found in caves in limestone areas.

more rounded, characteristics usually associated with *sapiens* fossils.

Although Heidelberg, Petralona, Vértesszöllös and Bilzingsleben resemble *Homo erectus* from Africa and Asia in may ways, they have a few more advanced features. The Steinheim skull and fragments of another skull found at Swanscombe in England are even more advanced. These skulls are considered to be 300,000 to 200,000 years old. Some experts have suggested that these fossils share features with a later, large-brained population of western Europe called Neanderthal Man. For them, Steinheim and Swanscombe represent a transitional stage between the earlier *erectus*-like fossils and the later, Neanderthal, type of *sapiens*.

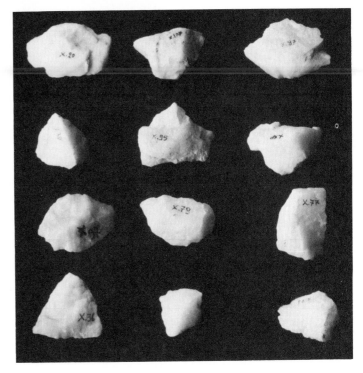

These small stones are tools. The edges have been chipped to form a cutting edge. They were made by Homo erectus *and found at Petralona.*

Middle Pleistocene Life

There are many sites from the Middle Pleistocene (1 million to 125,000 years ago) – more than from the Early Pleistocene – from which it is possible to reconstruct the lifestyle of contemporary hominids. The evidence from the Middle Pleistocene sites shows that *Homo erectus* was a highly successful hunter. At Choukoutien, in China, seventy per cent of the animal bones found are from deer, suggesting that Peking Man, the region's *Homo erectus*, had a taste for venison and was skillful at hunting for it. A site in Kenya contains the 400,000-year-old remains of over eighty baboons of all ages, suggesting that hominids may have killed an entire troop of these animals, which were much larger than modern ones.

Middle Pleistocene hominids were also capable of efficiently killing animals much larger than either deer or baboons. Sites at Torralba and Ambrona in central Spain show evidence of hunting for elephants and wild horses. How exactly the animals, driven by fire into the marsh, were killed is not known, but stones found in the area may have been used as missiles.

The large numbers of animals found at Torralba and Ambrona were not killed at one time. Each animal would have provided enough meat for a considerable group of hominids. Probably the animals were killed over successive seasons, when these Middle Pleistocene hunters returned to the area with the migrations of the game animals. Despite man's growing skill as a hunter, scientists believe that fruit, nuts and roots were still the mainstay of his diet.

Another Middle Pleistocene site, Terra Amata in

At Terra Amata in France, archaeologists found the remains of several primitive huts. This reconstruction shows what archaeologists think the hut looked like.

southern France, clearly records the pattern of living. Excavations revealed the remains of huts outlined in stones and holes that held supports for the structures. The position of these huts suggests that Terra Amata was occupied at least eleven different times.

Although no hominid fossil bones exist at Terra Amata, there is a single small footprint. The maker of this footprint would have been barely five feet tall. It is not known whether this was a child or a small adult. The size of the huts and the amount of food remains suggest that probably no more than twenty or twenty-five people lived there at any one time. The size of the site is consistent with evidence from the camps of present-day Bushmen in Africa, and Australian Aborigines, who still lead a primitive life hunting and gathering food.

The remains of a wooden bowl containing some lumps of ocher were found within one of the hut structures at Terra Amata. Ocher is a soft form of iron ore – yellow to brownish-red in color – that was used for body painting and cave painting, and also to sprinkle over the dead at the time of burial to give the corpse a life-like glow. Apart from this ocher, there is no apparent evidence of burial of the dead, of art, or of religious activity throughout the entire period.

Scientists do not know whether these early humans had language, but the way of life revealed by these sites suggests that they were able to speak. For example, it would be almost impossible for a group of hunters to trap and kill large animals without being able to communicate with one another. Hand signals could be used, but would be very impractical when hands were busy wielding weapons.

A present-day Bushman from southwest Africa starts to build a hut by making a circle of holes into which he puts tree branches. Archaeologists use surviving practices such as this in association with evidence from ancient sites to help them make reconstructions.

The Piltdown Hoax

The tale of Piltdown Man, the most famous forgery in the great detective story of the origins of man, began in 1912. On December 18 that year Charles Dawson, a well-known amateur British archaeologist, and Arthur Smith Woodward, of the British Museum of Natural History, announced the discovery of some amazing human fossils. The remains comprised nine pieces of skull, a broken jaw with two teeth in place, a few stone tools, and some animal bones, all of which had been found on a farm near Piltdown Common in Sussex, England.

When pieced together the skull looked distinctly human. Although Piltdown Man, as the hominid became known, had unusually thick bones, the brain case was large and rounded. There was no sign of prominent brow ridges or other apelike features. However, the shape of the jaw bone resembled that of an ape. The only human characteristic of this jaw was the wear on the two molars, which were ground down flat, as is frequently true of hominids who eat tough or abrasive foods, such as seeds. In other words the creature had the jaw of an ape and the skull of *Homo sapiens*.

The primitive stone tools found with these remains suggested a remote age for Piltdown Man, perhaps the Early Pleistocene or even the Late Pliocene. (In 1912 experts thought the Pliocene lasted from 1 million to 600,000 years ago. Scientists now date it to between 5 million and 1.7 million years ago.) This date was also supported by some animal bones found with Piltdown Man.

To most scientists of the time, Piltdown Man fulfilled a prediction made by the pioneering evolutionist Charles Darwin, who had believed that humans and the apes could be connected genetically through a still undiscovered creature. Most significantly, it was half human in precisely the feature that was then accepted as the most important difference between humans and the apes – the brain. At this time there was little fossil evidence to contradict the idea that the brain was among the first of the human features to evolve.

As time went on, however, additional *Homo erectus* fossils were found in Java and China, while in South Africa the australopithecines were being discovered. All these fossils had human-like jaws and teeth and relatively small brains in contrast to Piltdown Man's large brain and apelike jaw. The large brain simply did not fit with the rest of the fossil evidence. By 1948 scientists knew that bones buried in the earth gradually absorb fluorine. The older a bone, the more fluorine it contains. When the Piltdown materials were tested for fluorine, the skull and jaw fragments turned out to be much younger than the Early Pleistocene animal bones with which the skull had been found. The tests proved that Piltdown Man's

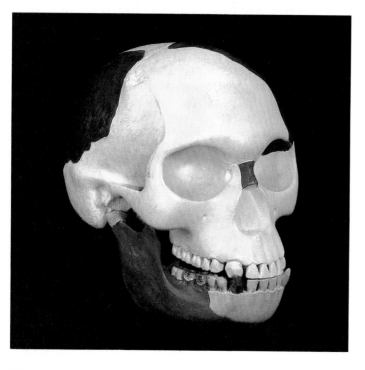

A cast of the skull remains called Piltdown Man. The dark-colored pieces are casts of the actual Piltdown bones, while the lighter-colored areas are reconstructions. The jaw was from a modern orangutan and the skull bones were no more than 500 years old.

The site in Sussex, England, where the Piltdown remains were found. In the foreground are Charles Dawson (left) and Arthur Smith Woodward, the two scientists who discovered Piltdown Man and published their findings in 1912.

bones were very much more recent than the Early Pleistocene animal bones with which it was found.

Scientists were now very suspicious. In 1953 all the Piltdown material was tested for its authenticity. Not only was the recent age of the jaw and skull confirmed, but the jaw proved to be that of a modern orangutan, with the teeth filed down to imitate wear on human teeth.

But the forger had not stopped there. A bone tool found with the remains had been made in recent times with a steel knife, which leaves different marks than does a stone flake or ax. The tools, as well as the animal bones, had been taken from different archaeological sites.

Once the forgery was exposed by modern scientific analysis the mystery was no longer where Piltdown Man came in human evolution but who was responsible for the hoax, and why? Although Dawson, the discoverer of most of the Piltdown material, is frequently singled out as the person responsible for this practical joke, there is no definite proof and the question is far from settled.

71

Man in Transition

It is difficult to define the exact point at which *Homo erectus* ends and *Homo sapiens* begins. Fossils of *Homo sapiens* have rounded skulls, thin bones, vertical foreheads, chins, and little or no brow ridges. The great majority of human skulls found throughout the world dating from about 40,000 or 30,000 years ago show these modern characteristics. Human fossils more than 400,000 years old clearly show the features of *Homo erectus* – thick bone, long low skulls, large brow ridges, and no chins.

Most of the fossils from between 400,000 and 40,000 years ago have features that are intermediate between these two definite species, making them difficult to classify. They are called archaic *Homo sapiens* because of their combination of characteristics from both the older *Homo erectus* and the younger *Homo sapiens*.

In Europe, in this transitional period, the fossils from Steinheim and Swanscombe, Mauer and Petralona, show the mixed features. In China there are three collections of well-preserved fossil material from between about 250,000 and 100,000 years ago. The first are remains of five or six individuals, now known as Hsuchiayao Man, found near Datong in Shensi Province. While these remains include many *Homo erectus* features, the backs of the skulls are more rounded and therefore more modern than *Homo erectus*. The second, the skull found near Shaochuan in Kwangtung Province, is more complete than that of Hsuchiayao Man. Although the skull is rounded, it has the thick bone and heavy brow ridges of the earlier *Homo erectus* type. Even more complete is the third, a skull from Dali in Shensi Province which was found in 1978. It preserves much of the face and shows a similar mixture of features.

In Africa, too, variations in form are found among the transitional fossils. The skull from Broken Hill, Zambia, is one of the best-preserved skulls ever excavated. It has the *Homo erectus* characteristics of a large, heavy face and big brow ridges. Unfortunately the site is difficult to date accurately, so although suggested dates vary between 300,000 and 100,000 years, nothing is certain. A skull from Ndutu, Tanzania, which may be as old as 400,000 years, has a modern vertical forehead behind its *Homo erectus* brow ridges. A well-preserved skull from the Ngaloba beds at Laetoli, shows a mixture of *Homo erectus* and *Homo sapiens* features. The top of the skull is expanded, in contrast to *Homo erectus* skulls. It has been dated at about 120,000 years.

Another skull of much more modern appearance from about 130,000 years ago is called Omo I after the site in southern Ethiopia where it was found. It is

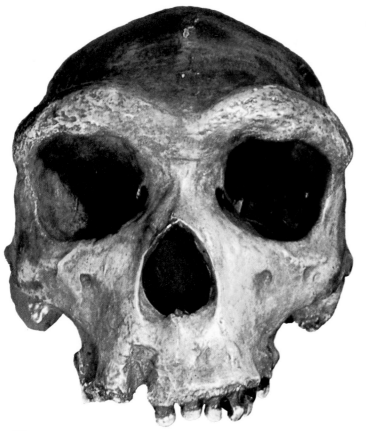

This skull from Broken Hill in Zambia, is one of the best preserved transitional fossils. It has Homo erectus *features, such as a large, heavy face and big brow ridges. The presence of decay in the teeth suggests that something sweet, perhaps honey, was part of the diet.*

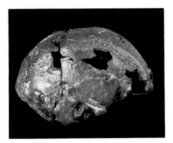

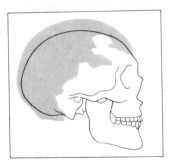

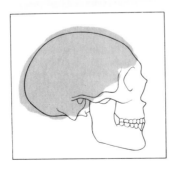

The fragmented remains discovered in 1974 in these excavations at Hsuchiayao in China's Shensi Province are thought to represent five or six individuals. They are probably 100,000 years old.

The so-called Omo I and Omo II skulls in the photograph (top left and right, above), were found in the Omo River valley. Despite their similar age – about 130,000 years – the skulls differ considerably. Omo I is rounded while Omo II is flatter as the comparisons with two present-day skulls show.

more rounded than in *Homo erectus*. A fragment of the lower jaw (not illustrated here) includes a modern jutting human chin, a feature not found in either *Homo erectus* or in many of the other archaic *Homo sapiens* remains.

Although most scientists agree that this skull shows more modern features than do other archaic *Homo sapiens* of its age, a second skull, found in the same deposits, is more like the other transitional African *Homo erectus* fossils. Known as Omo II, this skull is long and relatively flat. A keel or ridge runs along its top, and the back of the skull is most prominent at the level of the ear openings, although the skull is also fairly wide toward the top.

On present evidence the Omo I skull is the most modern of the transitional fossils. These few skulls and related fragments, however, do not provide enough well-dated material for anthropologists to draw positive conclusions about the arrival of *Homo sapiens*.

The Neanderthals

In 1856 in a limestone gorge called the Neander Valley near Düsseldorf in Germany, quarrymen uncovered some hominid remains. These fossils were the first recognized specimens of Neanderthal Man, a type of *Homo sapiens* that anthropologists believe lived primarily in Europe between about 150,000 and 31,000 years ago.

Although relatively modern, Neanderthal Man was different from living humans. The skull was long, with large, curving brow ridges over the eyes. The forehead sloped back sharply from these ridges, and at the back of the skull was a bulge called the occipital bun. Neanderthals also had sturdier arms and leg bones and much larger joints than modern humans. These features suggest that Neanderthal Man was probably more powerful than present-day humans.

When the bones of the first Neanderthal Man were discovered, Darwin had not yet published *The Origin of Species*. People were not yet thinking in terms of human evolution or the existence of hominid fossils, so the significance of the bones was not appreciated. However, by the turn of the century, after Darwin's ideas had spread, other Neanderthal remains were found in France, Belgium and Czechoslovakia, and recognized as being a type of early man.

Scientists in the early twentieth century put Neanderthal Man halfway between chimpanzees and modern humans in the evolutionary tree, but later study has completely disproved this. Although rugged in body form, Neanderthal Man was a very close relative of modern humans. The study of Neanderthal living-sites and tools points toward a successful life under the cold, harsh conditions of the last glacial period in Europe. His tools were more complex than those of *Homo erectus*, he was good at hunting large animals, and he regularly used fire.

Scientists today have noted that the Neanderthals seemed to be specifically adapted to a cold environment. They point to the short, stocky body that would help maintain a warm body temperature in cold conditions. The large nasal cavity within the relatively big nose would warm the inhaled air before it reached the lungs, and the large blood vessels supplying blood to the face would warm this area of the body.

Until recently the oldest Neanderthal fossils dated from the warm interlude before the last glacial period. However, discoveries at the sites of Biache, La Chaise, and Lazaret in France push the oldest evidence for Neanderthal Man back before 130,000

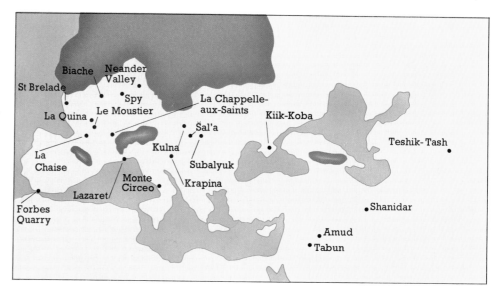

This map, indicating some of the major sites where Neanderthal fossils have been found, shows that Neanderthal Man was widely distributed throughout Europe and the Middle East. During the last glacial period, the Neanderthals of western Europe were isolated from the rest of the European continent by ice-sheets, and so formed a separate population.

years ago, which was during the next to last glacial advance. Neanderthal features have also been recognized in much earlier European fossils such as those from Steinheim and Swanscombe. From such evidence, and the fact that Neanderthal characteristics seem consistent with cold weather adaptation, scientists conclude that the first Neanderthals may have arisen during the harsh glacial conditions over a thousand centuries ago.

Neanderthal features have also been recognized in fossils of hominids contemporary with Neanderthal Man but outside Europe. Early human remains found at Shanidar in Iraq, and at Amud and Tabūn in Israel, show similarities with their European neighbors.

Neanderthal Man's precise position in evolution continues to be a puzzle, not least because there are no fossils outside Europe and southwest Asia that show typical Neanderthal features. Neanderthal Man would seem to be an extinct form of *Homo sapiens* that lived in this region during the last two major glacial advances.

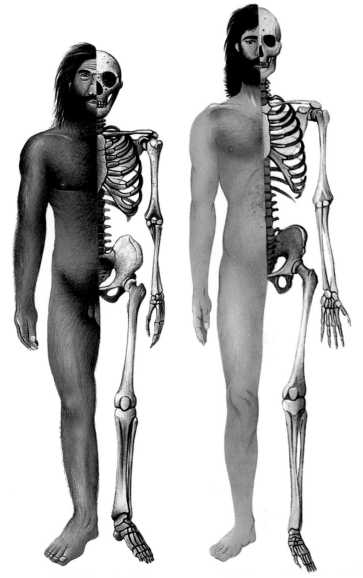

Neanderthal Man (above left) was stocky and muscular in comparison to modern man (above right). The size and shape of fossil bones, together with marks left on them by muscles and tendons, are all evidence of this.

These limb bones, vertebrae and skull (left) were found at the Neanderthal site of La-Chapelle-aux-Saints in France. They show typical Neanderthal features. For example, the skull is long with a sloping forehead and pronounced brow ridges, and the face has a particularly large nasal cavity. The femur, the fourth bone from the left, is particularly strongly-built. The bend in the upper arm bone (at far left in the picture) is unusual; it might have been caused by disease or a poor diet.

The Rise of the Cro-Magnons

About 30,000 years ago people almost identical in appearance to today's man were living in the limestone valleys and gorges of southern France that had been occupied by Neanderthal Man until about 31,000 years ago. Scientists called these people Cro-Magnon, after a rock shelter of that name near the village of Les Eyzies, in the Dordogne, France, where their remains were first discovered in 1868.

There are no known human fossils from western Europe that provide an evolutionary link between Neanderthal Man and the Cro-Magnon people. Even so, some scientists at first believed that Neanderthal Man was the direct ancestor of Cro-Magnon Man. They argued that this evolution was related to tool improvement. If Neanderthal Man used his teeth for holding and tearing objects, this could explain both the large projecting teeth and face, and the occipital bun, a bulge at the rear of the skull to which muscles were attached. The heavy muscles at the rear of the skull would counteract the stress on the teeth and face. As Neanderthal Man made better tools, he would have used his teeth less often, and so they may have become smaller. The face, too, would have become flatter and the back of the skull more rounded. So modern human beings might have emerged from a Neanderthal ancestry.

The majority of Neanderthal fossils are found together with tools that belong to a tool industry called the Mousterian, after Le Moustier, a cave in the Dordogne, France, where it was first identified. Typical Mousterian tools, which date from 100,000 to 35,000 years ago, include scrapers, spearpoints and borers made from thin stone flakes chipped off a larger stone called a core. The tools found with Cro-Magnon remains – such as single-edged knives and graceful leaf-shaped spearpoints – are more finely worked and made from flakes, called blades.

Looking at the different types of tools is not a very useful means of defining the relationship of these two

These two stones show a typical method of making Mousterian tools. On the left is a large stone termed a core. It was struck with another stone to form small flakes, like the one on the right. The edges of the flakes were then sharpened to make good cutting tools. One big core could provide a large number of flake tools.

human types because more modern skulls were found at the Israeli sites of Skhūl and Jebel Qafze together with tools of the earlier Mousterian culture. At St. Cézaire in France Neanderthal remains were found with Chatelperronian tools (from Chatelperron, a site in central France) which blend features of Mousterian tools and tools used by Cro-Magnons.

Scientists can therefore no longer claim that the transition of Neanderthal Man into Cro-Magnon Man is necessarily related to changing tool cultures. Equally, because the evidence now suggests that Neanderthal Man overlapped with Cro-Magnon Man in western Europe, the Neanderthals could not be direct ancestors of the first Cro-Magnon people.

But why did Neanderthal Man disappear so com-

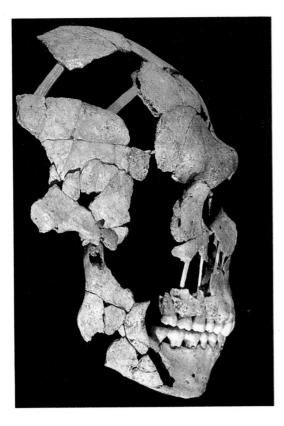

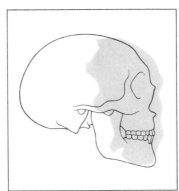

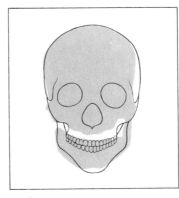

This Neanderthal skull from St Cézaire, France, is dated to 34,000–31,000 years ago – the most recent Neanderthal fossil known. The skull's Neanderthal features are obvious when it is superimposed on the outline of a modern human skull (center top). The forehead is low and sloping, the face projects and the brow ridges are well-developed.

The skull of Cro-Magnon Man is virtually indistinguishable in shape and features from that of modern man, as seen when they are superimposed on each other (center above). The Cro-Magnon skull has no brow ridges and shows other modern features, such as a high forehead and a smoothly rounded braincase.

pletely? As Cro-Magnon Man spread across Europe from southwest Asia these two races must have come into contact, if not conflict. Perhaps Cro-Magnon Man brought with him diseases to which the Neanderthals were not immune. This may have been the cause of the Neanderthals' extinction, just as many isolated tribes in the last few centuries have died out through contact with diseases brought by explorers. Or perhaps Cro-Magnon Man was just more efficient at obtaining food. But there is no reliable evidence that Neanderthal Man was less intelligent than Cro-Magnon Man. In fact, some Neanderthals' skulls held larger brains than those of Cro-Magnon Man. Until more evidence is available, the mystery of the Neanderthals' disappearance remains.

This stone handax is a typical example of a Mousterian tool. It was made sometime between 100,000–40,000 years ago by one of the Neanderthal peoples. The stone has been carefully worked around the edges to make a sharp and efficient tool.

Life in the Last Ice Age

Both Neanderthal and Cro-Magnon Man lived in the cold conditions of the last major glacial period. During the greatest cold periods (about 58,000 to 40,000, and 29,000 to 13,000 years ago) one ice sheet extended into present-day Poland, Germany, and northern France. Ice also covered Britain and the mountainous regions of southern Europe. In spite of the bitter cold, the environment was not completely hostile. The tundra that made up the remaining landscape supported large herds of deer and wild horses, as well as mammoths and woolly rhinoceroses.

Some scientists believe that the harsh and bleak life of Ice Age people was connected with the first appearance in human society of the burial of the dead. The first definite evidence of this distinctively human practice comes from Neanderthal Man. At the site of Le Moustier in France the body of an adolescent Neanderthal boy was buried in a cave about 50,000 years ago. He had been laid on his side with his legs slightly bent. His head rested on his forearm on a pillow of flints, and near his hand was a beautifully made stone ax. Also in the grave were charred bones – perhaps an offering of roasted meat for his journey into the afterlife.

A similar grave exists at the site of Teshik-Tash in central Asia. Here the horns of ibex – a kind of mountain goat – were stuck in the ground around the head of the human skeleton.

There are many examples of similar burials at Neanderthal sites. Although anthropologists cannot explain what burial meant to the Neanderthals, such behavior and especially the presence of food remains suggests they may have developed a concept of the afterlife.

The Neanderthal peoples lived in small groups and hunted single animals, as had their Middle Pleistocene ancestors before them. However, with the appearance of the Cro-Magnon peoples, both group size and the hunting pattern changed. At

This burial scene is reconstructed from archaeological evidence from the Neanderthal site of Le Moustier, France. The relatives of the dead youth place food and tools in his grave, which suggests the Neanderthals had a form of religion.

Prědmost in Czechoslovakia a Cro-Magnon site contains the remains of large huts, a big communal grave, and the bones of at least 600 woolly mammoths. In southern France, at the site of Le Solutré, are the skeletons of some 10,000 wild horses. Anthropologists originally concluded that the Cro-Magnon hunters had to feed and clothe many people, judging from the size of the kill. Recent research suggests, however, that the animals were not individually butchered. The Cro-Magnon hunters may have either stampeded the herds over the cliff top, or else trapped them against

One of the major game animals hunted by both Neanderthal and Cro-Magnon peoples was the now-extinct mammoth, of which this remarkably preserved baby (right) is a fine specimen. Found in Siberia, the permafrost – the layer of permanently frozen soil – in which it was buried had acted as a natural deep freeze, keeping this 10,000-year-old creature almost intact.

the base of the cliff. The hunters then took only what meat and skins they needed.

The peoples of Prědmost and Le Solutré lived during the end of the last major glacial period. But as the temperature rose and the glaciers retreated, the melting ice created an indirect benefit. The sea level rose, producing shallower and warmer coastal waters, slow-running rivers, and estuaries. These conditions attracted migratory birds in great numbers and allowed fish to swim up the rivers. As a result the hominids had a reliable supply of food. They were no longer dependent on hunting animals. This allowed man's population to expand as never before.

The vast collections of animal remains found at such Cro-Magnon sites as Prědmost in Czechoslovakia indicate that these people were skilful hunters, as this reconstruction of a hunting scene suggests.

Artists of the Caves

Although earlier Cro-Magnon people produced cave art, most of the 125 known European art caves date from the end of the last glacial period, and were the work of the later Cro-Magnon peoples. Prehistoric paintings have survived in caves because they are protected from the weather. There is evidence that rock walls and overhangs near living-sites were also painted. For example, broken pieces of rock painted red and black have been found at Abri Pataud in southern France. These pieces had broken off a nearby wall – remains, perhaps, of a mural. There are also carvings of animals on cave walls, and three-dimensional sculptures. Small, stylized figures of human females, known as Venus figurines, are found in many living-sites, particularly in eastern Europe. And the remains of what might have been a sculptor's workshop were discovered at Dolni Věstonice in Czechoslovakia. Scattered around a large fire hearth at this campsite, in various stages of preparation, were many small clay animals.

This prehistoric art may be more than just decoration. Much of it lies in remote and inaccessible cave areas. In the French Pyrenees, in the Tuc d'Audoubert cave, two clay sculptures of bison were found in the center of a circular cave room far from the entrance. Near the bison a circle of small human heelprints was found. Were children led into this chamber, perhaps for an initiation ceremony? The answer will never be known for certain.

In many of the caves animal pictures are painted on top of one another. It is known that until very recently, Aborigines in some areas of Australia painted pictures of animals in a similar fashion on sacred rock walls. They were preparing themselves for a successful hunt. Perhaps this was the purpose of some Cro-Magnon art.

These bison, modeled in the Tuc d'Audoubert cave, Ariège, France, date to between 17,000 and 12,000 years ago. The cave artists often made use of the shapes of the rock formations in the caves they were decorating to give the animals a more lifelike appearance.

These paintings of deer from a cave at Lascaux, France, date to between 22,000 and 18,000 years ago. No one knows what such paintings mean, but Cro-Magnon people may have painted pictures of animals on sacred cave walls to ensure good hunting.

Many of the painted animals appear pregnant. As the last glacial period drew to a close and the temperature rose, the main source of food, the large herds of animals used to the cold, began to decrease. These paintings of pregnant animals may have been meant symbolically to increase the herds' fertility. The Venus figurines too may have been fertility symbols, for they have exaggerated breasts and buttocks while the rest of their anatomy is only suggested.

Certain series of dots and parallel lines scratched on pieces of bone and ivory may be calendars based on the phases of the moon. To Cro-Magnon people, observing the skies and predicting the seasons would have been a natural thing to do. Some scientists have suggested that plants, animals, fish, and fowl found in paintings and sculpture depicted seasonal rituals. A stone shrine found in a cave near Santander, Spain, in 1981 suggests that the people living there 14,000 years ago had a formalized religion.

The golden period for ice age art came to an end about 12,000 years ago, probably due to the continued warming of the environment. Forest replaced tundra, and the large herds of game animals, the staple food, disappeared. The hunters either followed the game animals north or moved to the coast where they could live on fish and other seafood.

Homo sapiens in Africa and Asia

The appearance of *Homo sapiens* in Europe is only one small part of the story of human evolution. Scientists know that Cro-Magnon men had evolved before entering Europe about 35,000 to 30,000 years ago, but the evidence of where this evolution occurred is poor.

Early peoples entering western Europe probably used the convenient land routes from southwest Asia. It has been suggested that they may also have originated in that area, although the evidence of human evolution in southwest Asia at the time of the European Neanderthals is complicated. Neanderthal fossils are known from the cave of Shanidar in Iraq, dated between 60,000 and 30,000 years ago, and from the cave of Tabūn in Israel, dated to about 45,000 years ago. But skeletons found only a few hundred yards from Tabūn, in the cave of Skhūl, and dated as old as 40,000 years are more modern in form. Remains from another site in Israel, Jebel Qafze, are similar in form to those from Skhūl and about the same age.

Curiously, some of the skulls from the sites of Skhūl and Jebel Qafze have slight brow ridges and other Neanderthal-like features. Some scientists have, therefore, suggested that these remains represent an intermediate stage in a gradual evolution from Neanderthals to modern *Homo sapiens*. However, recent detailed analysis has convinced many experts that in spite of their primitive features the fossils from Skhūl and Jebel Qafze are true *Homo sapiens*. If this is so, the few thousand years separating the Neanderthal fossils of the region from those of the modern peoples are hardly sufficient for such evolution to have occurred. Thus the mystery remains. If the modern *Homo sapiens* found in southwest Asia did not originate there, where did they come from?

In Africa, skulls of completely modern appearance are difficult to date. For example, the Fish Hoek skull from South Africa may be as old as 40,000 to 35,000 years or as recent as 18,500 years. This ambiguity

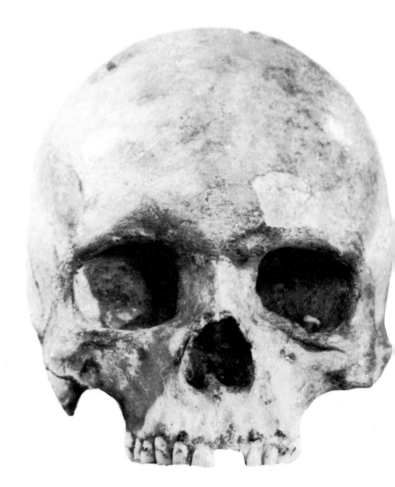

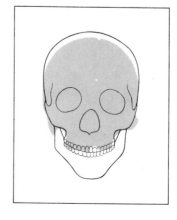

Liujiang Man is the name given to the skull shown above. About 40,000 years old, it is the oldest anatomically modern skull yet discovered in China. The diagram at left compares the fossil remains (shown in gray) with a modern skull (outlined in black).

arises from the presence of two stone tool cultures at the Fish Hoek site, and scientists are uncertain to which culture the skull belongs. Deposits surrounding apparently modern skull fragments from Border Cave on the boundary between Swaziland and South Africa, suggest that these fossils may date to between 90,000 and 50,000 years ago. Fragmentary human remains from the Klasies River site in South Africa show none of the heavy features of the African archaic *Homo sapiens*, and these remains may be at least 90,000 years old.

The fossil evidence in Asia is also inconclusive. The earliest known completely modern *Homo sapiens* in Asia dates to 40,000 years ago, and there is no apparent link between this material and earlier Asian populations. A skull from Niah in Sarawak and another from Liujiang in China are both of this age, and two skulls from Wadjak in Java also may be of the same date.

If the African fossils prove to be as old as they might be, it could mean that the first completely modern human beings appeared not far from where their distant ancestors, the australopithecines, first appeared. According to this hypothesis, a group of archaic *Homo sapiens* in Africa evolved modern human skeletal characteristics and then spread throughout the world. If the African fossils prove to be younger, it could mean that today's *Homo sapiens* gradually arose at the same time in Africa and Asia from different groups of archaic *Homo sapiens*. The answers must await further fossil discoveries.

The entrance to the Niah Cave in Sarawak, Malaysia, photographed from inside the cave. A skull – known as Niah Man – found at this site is one of the oldest skulls that is similar to those of the people who live in the region today.

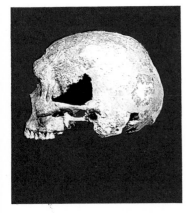 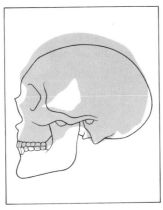

The best-preserved skull (far left) of the eleven hominids found at Jebel Qafze, Israel. This is the earliest representative of modern human beings found in the Middle East. The gray area in the diagram on the far left shows this skull in relation to that of a modern human skull, which is outlined in black.

The Southern Migration

Late in 1979 an extremely interesting skull was found at Cossack in Western Australia. It was that of a male who, from dental and other evidence, was about forty years old at death, and who lived as recently as 6500 years ago. It is an important skull because at this late date it shows features very different from those of populations living at the same time elsewhere in the world. The skull is long, the forehead slopes sharply backward, the face is large and projecting with well-developed brow ridges. Also, the skull bones are very thick – as in *Homo erectus* and some of the oldest *Homo sapiens* peoples.

The skull is similar in form to those of heavily built hominids from southeast Australia, which range in age between about 10,000 and 6000 years. The site of Kow Swamp in southeast Australia has produced remains of forty individuals of this type from 10,000 years ago. Others were found at sites in Talgai and Mossgiel. However, mixed in with this group are other Australian human skulls that are more lightly built and rounded. These remains range in age from 26,000 years to 6000 years ago. These two types of fossils clearly suggest that there was greater variation in human skull form in Australia at this time than in other areas of the world.

In Africa, on the other hand, all the human fossils dating from this same period look like the skulls of living humans in form. They include 11,000-year-old remains from western Nigeria, others from the Sahara which are 6400 years old, and some from the Kenya highlands of about 10,000 to 8000 years of age. The skulls are very similar to those of the populations occupying these areas today, while the earlier remains from South Africa show similarities to those of the present-day !Kung. In China, too, the one skull from Liujiang and those found in the upper cave at Choukoutien are also modern in form and resemble the skulls of present-day oriental peoples. Finally, in Europe, the Cro-Magnon remains look like those of present-day Europeans.

The two different Australian populations may have entered Australia by two different migration routes as early as 40,000 years ago. The skulls with light, rounded features are similar in form to modern Chinese skulls. They may have come to Australia via Indochina, Borneo, and New Guinea. The heavily built group, which shows many similarities with archaic *Homo sapiens* specimens from Java, may have come to Australia via the Indonesian island of Timor. Land bridges connected New Guinea to Australia and Borneo to Indochina, at this time, but they did not join Australia to Timor or mainland Asia. Thus, both of these peoples had to cross at least 50 miles of sea to reach Australia, presumably in primitive boats – a journey requiring skill and intelligence.

It seems that at least three different peoples lived just before 40,000 years ago: Neanderthal Man in Europe, the parent population of the Cossack and other heavily-built Australian peoples in southern Asia, and the peoples with modern skulls in Africa and Asia.

The massive skull (below left) was found at Cossack, Western Australia. When it is superimposed (gray) on the outline of a modern skull (in black, below right), such primitive features as the projecting face and heavy brow ridges are very obvious.

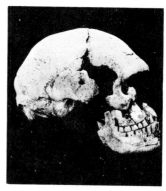

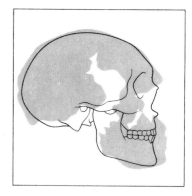

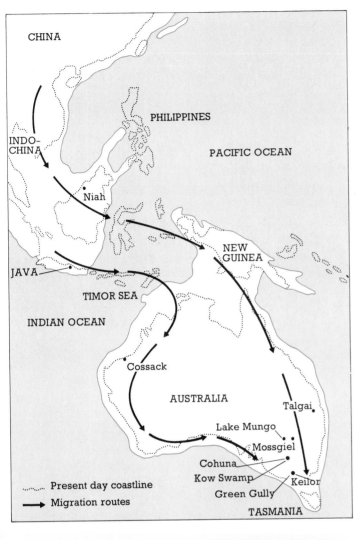

Man probably reached Australia from southeast Asia by two different routes, as this map shows. The lightly-built population came through New Guinea, while the more strongly-built people may have taken a more southerly route and entered Australia from Java.

A group of Australian Aborigines rests beside a river in central Australia. These people still live as hunter-gatherers, one of very few groups left in the world who follow this way of life today.

This skeleton from the Lake Mungo region of Australia is shown here as it was uncovered during excavation. It is the remains of one of the lightly-built race of Australians.

Man in the New World

In body form and skeletal details the present-day monkeys of Central and South America are different from the monkeys of Africa and Asia, from the apes, and from modern human beings. This suggests that there is no evolutionary link between the New World monkeys and man. It also indicates that the evolutionary roots of modern peoples lie in Africa and Eurasia, and not in the Americas. This view is further borne out by the fact that no fossils of humans before *Homo sapiens* have been found in the New World. At some time in the past, therefore, the ancestors of native Americans must have made their way from the Old World to the New. The physical resemblance between northeast Asian peoples and the native Americans suggests this.

At various times throughout the Pleistocene epoch, North America was connected to Asia by a land-bridge that stretched across the Bering Strait, a shallow body of water separating Alaska from Siberia. But it was probably not until the last major glacial period, beginning about 100,000 years ago, that human intelligence and culture had advanced enough for hominids to cope with the cold climate in the region of the Bering Strait landbridge.

There are two principal theories about when human beings reached the New World. Some archaeological sites in North America are dated between 11,500 and 10,000 years ago, and show signs that the people living there were successful hunters. Many of the sites also contain bones of mammal species that became extinct at about the same time. Perhaps the extinction of the animals was caused by over-hunting. In South America, one of the most important sites, Fell's Cave in Patagonia, Chile, shows

evidence that human populations had reached the southern-most tip of the Americas by about 10,000 years ago. Some scientists believe that a thousand years would have been sufficient time for human populations to spread from Canada to the southern tip of South America through the pressure of increased populations rather than deliberate migration.

Other scientists disagree with this theory and believe that man entered the Americas at an earlier date. They argue that the cultures of early Americans vary tremendously, for instance in their hunting techniques, and that such great differences almost certainly took more than a thousand years to develop. This theory is supported by the growing body of archaeological evidence that points more and more toward the conclusion that human populations were in both North and South America much earlier than

This complete ground sloth skeleton was assembled from remains found in tar pits at Rancho La Brea, California. These sloths were about six feet tall. They became extinct about 10,000 years ago.

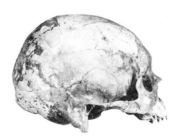

This skull comes from La Jolla in southern California and has been dated at 44,000 years old although this dating is now thought to be controversial.

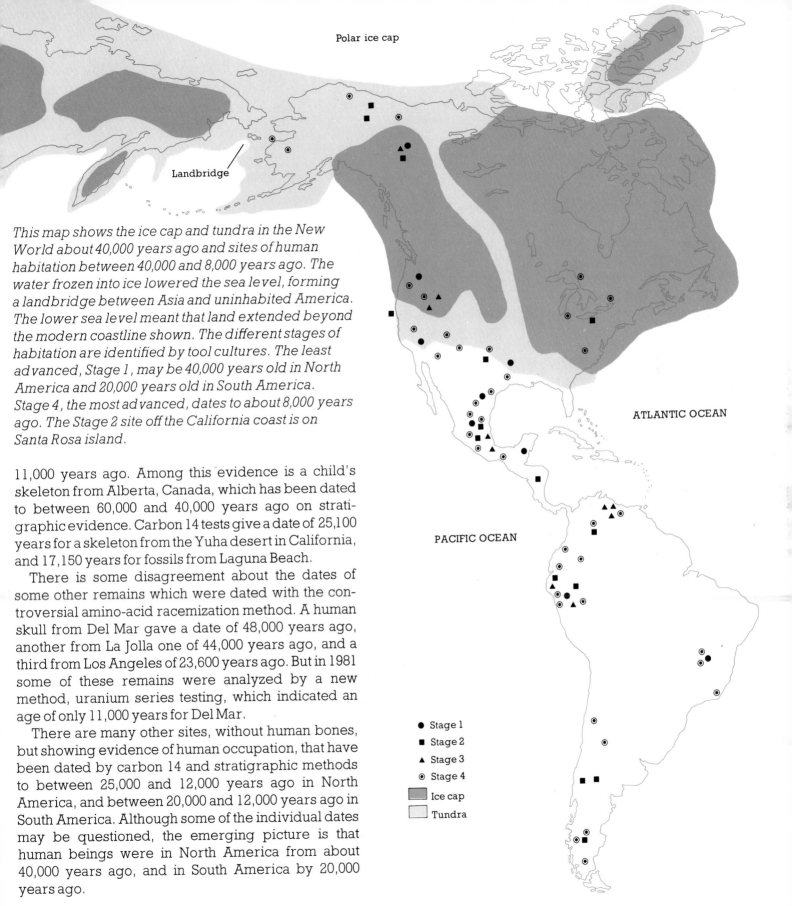

Polar ice cap

Landbridge

This map shows the ice cap and tundra in the New World about 40,000 years ago and sites of human habitation between 40,000 and 8,000 years ago. The water frozen into ice lowered the sea level, forming a landbridge between Asia and uninhabited America. The lower sea level meant that land extended beyond the modern coastline shown. The different stages of habitation are identified by tool cultures. The least advanced, Stage 1, may be 40,000 years old in North America and 20,000 years old in South America. Stage 4, the most advanced, dates to about 8,000 years ago. The Stage 2 site off the California coast is on Santa Rosa island.

ATLANTIC OCEAN

PACIFIC OCEAN

● Stage 1
■ Stage 2
▲ Stage 3
◉ Stage 4
▨ Ice cap
▧ Tundra

11,000 years ago. Among this evidence is a child's skeleton from Alberta, Canada, which has been dated to between 60,000 and 40,000 years ago on stratigraphic evidence. Carbon 14 tests give a date of 25,100 years for a skeleton from the Yuha desert in California, and 17,150 years for fossils from Laguna Beach.

There is some disagreement about the dates of some other remains which were dated with the controversial amino-acid racemization method. A human skull from Del Mar gave a date of 48,000 years ago, another from La Jolla one of 44,000 years ago, and a third from Los Angeles of 23,600 years ago. But in 1981 some of these remains were analyzed by a new method, uranium series testing, which indicated an age of only 11,000 years for Del Mar.

There are many other sites, without human bones, but showing evidence of human occupation, that have been dated by carbon 14 and stratigraphic methods to between 25,000 and 12,000 years ago in North America, and between 20,000 and 12,000 years ago in South America. Although some of the individual dates may be questioned, the emerging picture is that human beings were in North America from about 40,000 years ago, and in South America by 20,000 years ago.

Present-Day Hunters and Gatherers

There are still people who hunt and gather wild foods as their sole means of subsistence, as anthropologists think man's early ancestors might have done. These living hunters and gatherers generally occupy areas that are either remote or unsuitable for agriculture, such as Alaska, Greenland, and northern Canada; the tropical forests of South America, Africa, and Asia; and the deserts of southern Africa and Australia. Studying the lifestyles of these people can provide clues to the lifestyle of man's ancestors. However, in drawing parallels between living hunter-gatherers and human ancestors it is important to remember that *Homo sapiens* evolved while hunting and gathering was the universal way of life. Present-day hunters and gatherers are, therefore, only primitive in the sense that they have retained the hunting and gathering lifestyle of earlier ages.

The study of these hunters and gatherers has shown that their lifestyle is not always a harsh struggle for existence. For example, the !Kung people of the Kalahari Desert of Botswana and South Africa hunt and gather only two or three days a week. They spend the rest of the time visiting, entertaining, dancing, and storytelling. Of course this pattern of maximum leisure, which is also found among other hunters and gatherers of today, depends on sufficient food being available.

Plants are the staple food for these and other hunter-gatherers living in warm temperate to tropical areas of the world. Seeds, roots and fruit comprise sixty to eighty per cent of their total food by weight. Gathering plant food is more reliable than hunting, which involves chance. Among the !Kung people as well as among other similar peoples, gathering is primarily the women's activity while hunting is the men's. In fact, the men provide only a half to a third as much food as the women.

In the cool to cold temperate latitudes fishing – another reliable food source – is the chief activity.

A child of a tribe of bushmen from southern Africa lays a trap for a bird called the nightjar, which laid these eggs. He leaves one egg on the nest, makes a noose from fibers of the sanseveria plant and puts the other egg beyond the noose. When the bird returns to the nest it will stick its neck through the noose, while trying to recover the second egg.

An Eskimo fishing from an ice floe in northwest Greenland. Until the 1940s Eskimos hunted and fished with their traditional weapons – spears, harpoons, and hooks and lines. Today they use highly sophisticated modern equipment for hunting, including rifles, explosive charges and power boats when the ice has thawed.

Only in northern latitudes lying more than sixty degrees from the Equator is hunting more important than fishing or gathering plant foods. There, life may be correspondingly less secure.

The use of plant food provides a clue to the understanding of early human evolution. Although animal bones are preserved in human living-sites two million years old, perishable plant foods probably played a more important part in early man's diet. The key to early human evolution lies in the development of food sharing rather than in the development of hunting. Humans are the only mammals regularly to share all their food. This enables an entire group to benefit from the food procuring abilities of a few.

The size of a group depends on the available resources. Among the !Kung, the group structure is also dependent on water. Single camps around waterholes average about twenty people. This figure is characteristic of many hunting and gathering groups, and is also related to the number of people that can be supported on the food within a reasonable walking distance from camp. As food resources vary, however, the size of the groups also varies. Eskimos, for example, spend most of their time in small, single-family groups, but come together in larger groups when food supplies are abundant.

Flowers provide the Tasady people (far left) of the Philippine Islands with many of the minerals and vitamins essential to a healthy diet.

Edible roots form an important part of the diet of hunter-gatherers. The Amazonian Indian (left) searches in the thick undergrowth of the forest around his camp for roots to take back to the rest of the group.

Modern Peoples

The major differences recognized today between modern peoples throughout the world are body size and shape, hair type, facial form, and skin color. All these features are important, or have been in the past, for adaptation to different environments.

Skin and hair do not fossilize, so scientists can only speculate about the skin color of the Pliocene and Pleistocene hominids. As long as man's ancestors retained their covering of hair, their skin color would probably not have had any importance to their survival. But as they shed this protective coat, their skin would have been directly exposed to the sun in the savanna or other open environment. Almost certainly some adaptations were required to protect the skin against the effects of serious sunburn. The skin pigment melanin is a natural protection against

This couple on Waikiki Beach, Hawaii, have naturally pale skins – as the untanned areas show. Pale skins are found in peoples living in temperate regions where sunlight is less intense than in the tropics. In tropical climates pale skins generally develop tans as a protection against the sun.

sunburn because it inhibits the penetration of some of the ultraviolet rays that cause sunburn. This pigment is present to a greater degree in dark skin. Not surprisingly, modern peoples of Africa, southern India, and Australia, who have lived with the tropical sun for hundreds of generations, all have dark skin. Most probably, the first hominids to do without a coat of hair had dark skin also.

White skin is probably a relatively recent evolutionary development, possibly resulting from the movement of human beings into more northern and cloudy climates. Vitamin D, necessary for proper bone growth, is produced in the deep layers of the skin through the action of the ultraviolet rays. But further from the tropics, more of the sun's ultraviolet rays are filtered out by the earth's atmosphere. Sunburn is no longer a serious threat, but a deficiency of Vitamin D is. In fact, many Neanderthal fossils show evidence of bone deformities that may indicate a shortage of the vitamin. It is possible that light skin evolved to maintain the ideal level of Vitamin D.

There are exceptions to the general rule that dark-skinned peoples are native to the tropical regions and light-skinned to the temperate regions. In the Americas, for example, there is very little difference in pigmentation between peoples living along the length of the two continents – which comprise tropical, temperate, and arctic regions. But most of these exceptions can be explained by relatively recent migrations from other areas. Most evidence supports the conclusion that light and dark skins evolved in response to varying exposures to the ultraviolet rays of the sun.

The human body loses heat by radiation in association with sweat evaporation through the skin. Differences in the size and proportions of the human body are probably related to this natural system of temperature regulation. In hot climates people are generally slender and either small or tall. These physical types are ideally suited to such climates because each has a large skin surface relative to body volume, thus ensuring maximum heat loss. People in cold climates, however, need to conserve body heat. Therefore, they tend to have heavier, stockier bodies that minimize heat loss because of the relatively small skin area.

Facial form is also important in adaptation. The oriental face is generally thought to have developed in the cold conditions of the last glacial period. The broad, flat face with small ears and fat pads around the eyes is well suited to cold weather. The small nose and ears minimize heat loss here and prevent frostbite. The fat pads around the eyes protect them from damage by cold. The fact that people in the warmer parts of Asia, as well as in the Americas, have these oriental features is probably the result of relatively recent movements of oriental people into these areas.

Because these features that distinguish modern peoples were adaptations to different environments, and because humans have moved and interbred throughout the world, it is impossible to say how many distinct types of people exist today.

Over hundreds of generations man can adapt to his surroundings as this Dinka couple from the Sudan (below right) and the Lapps (below) show. The Dinkas live in a hot climate and their tall, slender bodies have a large area of skin in relation to body weight, thus ensuring the maximum surface through which heat is lost to keep the body cool. The Lapps, who live in a cold climate, have short, stocky bodies to minimize the surface through which heat is lost.

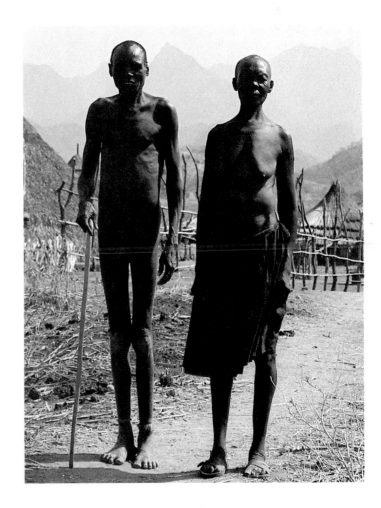

The Unending Search

Since Charles Darwin first suggested that the human species was the result of evolution, scientists have tried to answer the central question: what species preceded man? Many answers have been advanced since Darwin's theory appeared in print in 1859.

The first generally acknowledged fossil relevant to the question of man's origins – that of Neanderthal Man discovered in 1856 – was the subject of much controversy. Few were willing to grant this creature ancestor status, for in those days, the generally accepted belief was that any form of man found must look like present-day man.

As the decades passed, other fossils were discovered. Each of those discoveries considered to be more man-like than anything else previously found was, for a time, considered the answer to that critical question: who was man's ancestor? However, as more people became involved in the search for man's origins, the scientific techniques used to analyze their discoveries became increasingly complex. Each candidate put forward as man's ancestor became the focus of intense analysis and debate. And just when one discoverer announced *the* answer, another anthropologist would publicize a new fossil, a contradictory piece of evidence, or a well-reasoned dissenting opinion.

The search for man's origins, however, continued. Since the early 1960s anthropologists working in India and Pakistan, the island of Java, the vast reaches of China, and at least a dozen different sites in Africa have turned up literally thousands of fossilized hominid fragments thought to be the ancestor of man. Precisely who these fragments belong to and how closely these various ancient hominids relate to present-day men are controversial issues.

By now, many anthropologists realize that recovering a hominid fossil no longer completely answers questions of man's origins. It is, of course, a very necessary step since the work of the geologist, the anatomist, the paleontologist and the archaeologist – to name but a few of the more prominent specialists – cannot begin until the fossil has been found. And until the specialists have had their chance to analyze and compare, there is little any one can say conclusively about a badly fragmented section of skull or a tiny jaw fragment with a tooth or two in place.

Today there is much cooperation and interchange between specialists. Thus the expert in bipedalism or early hominid teeth is familiar with the key finds from a number of sites. The laboratory that dates the Omo rocks is also familiar with those from Koobi Fora, Laetoli and Hadar.

Over the past two decades, a number of chemists and molecular biologists have been addressing the question of man's origins without ever examining a single piece of fossilized bone or rock. These scientists believe that the genetic material common to man and his closest relative, the gorilla and the chimpanzee, will provide definitive answers about when men and the great apes separated to follow different evolutionary paths. Once this date is known, it will be relatively easy to narrow the field of potential ancestors. But it will not solve – for once and for all – the question of man's origins. There are always new theories to be explored, another site to excavate, even a previously classified fossil to re-examine.

In fact, it is this never-ending search for another piece of evidence that keeps the question of man's origins forever open. The answers – at least for the time being – may well be just another set of questions.

The Neanderthal skull known as Shanidar I lies in the earth of the Iraqi cave where it and other fossils recovered from this extremely productive site had been buried for at least 45,000 years. To anthropologists the find reveals much about the life of early man. Analysis of this skull and the skeleton found with it, for example, indicated that Shanidar I was born with a deformed arm and was blind in one eye before he died. Apparently the people of Shanidar cared enough to provide for those who could not take care of themselves.

Glossary

Absolute dating: determining the age in years of a fossil or the rock in which it is found. Methods of absolute dating include carbon 14, potassium-argon and fission track dating.

Acheulian culture: a stone tool culture, also known as industry, found in Africa, Europe, western Asia, and parts of India, that lasted from more than 1.2 million to about 200,000 years ago. Its characteristic tool was the handax.

Anthropology: the study of the science of mankind, which is divided into four principal categories: physical anthropology, the study of human evolution and variation in modern people; social anthropology, the study of human culture; archaeology, the study of the material remains and lifestyles of human groups that no longer exist; and linguistics, the study of language, its origins and development

Archaic *Homo sapiens*: the name given to those fossils found in Africa, Asia, Europe and Australia with features intermediate between *Homo erectus* and the more modern *Homo sapiens*

Australopithecine: pertaining to, a member of, or a feature typical of one of the forms of *Australopithecus*

Australopithecus afarensis: a species of australopithecine found in the Afar region of Ethiopia and Laetoli, in Tanzania. Some scientists dispute this name and assign these fossils to either another species of *Australopithecus* or an early form of *Homo*.

Australopithecus africanus: the name given to the Taung skull found in 1924 and from that date to other similar australopithecine fossils

Australopithecus boisei: the name given to an extremely large form of australopithecine which had jaws and teeth adapted to a vegetarian diet; generally thought to represent a sidebranch of the hominid evolutionary line

Australopithecus robustus: a species of australopithecine more lightly built than *boisei* but larger than *africanus*

Binominal nomenclature: the scientific system of giving plants and animals Latin names for both their genus and species

Bipedal locomotion, bipedalism: two-footed walking, especially in the upright, human fashion

Chatelperronian culture: a stone tool culture covering the period of about 34,000 to 31,000 years ago, that is believed by some to have developed in western Europe directly out of the earlier Mousterian culture

Classification: a system of categories by which scientists attempt to show the relationships between organisms

Cro-Magnon Man: a variety of modern European human being that lived in Europe from about 30,000 to 12,000 years ago

Culture: the term used to describe any made artifact or implement such as tools or weapons; also refers to human behavior characterized by the ability to speak and the ability to mold and control the environment

Early *Homo*: early representatives thought to belong to the genus *Homo*, living primarily in Africa between about 2 million and 1.5 million years ago, and perhaps much earlier. Some anthropologists prefer this name to the frequently used *Homo habilis*; others continue to classify these particular fossils as *Australopithecus*.

Evolution: the process by which all animals and plants have gradually changed in form over generations in order to adapt to their environment

Fossil: any preserved evidence of prehistoric animals and plants

Genus: a group of closely related species having a common ancestor

Hominid: any member of the human line of evolution since its separation from the line that leads to the modern apes, that is *Homo*, *Australopithecus*, and possibly *Ramapithecus*

Homo erectus: a species of hominid, thought to be the direct ancestor of man, that lived in Africa, Asia, and perhaps Europe between 1.5 million and 300,000 years ago

Homo habilis: a species of hominid represented primarily from Olduvai Gorge in East Africa in the period between 2 million and 1.5 million years ago; also known as early *Homo*

Homo sapiens: the scientific name for modern human beings

Human: relating to, or being characteristic of, man

Java Man: hominid fossils from Java that belong to the species *Homo erectus*; originally called *Pithecanthropus erectus*

Mousterian culture: a stone tool culture dating to between 100,000 and about 34,000 years ago, found primarily in Europe and southwest Asia

Natural selection: a process of evolution whereby the individuals in any one generation that are best adapted to their environment survive to breed and pass on their features to the next generation

Neanderthal Man: a form of hominid that lived primarily in western Europe but also east to Iraq between about 150,000 and 31,000 years ago. It may be a direct human ancestor, but scientists remain uncertain about this.

Paleontology: the study of ancient life revealed by fossil material

Peking Man: hominid fossils, found at Choukoutien in China, that belong to the species *Homo erectus*; originally called *Sinanthropus pekinensis*

Pithecanthropus erectus: an early name given to Java Man, now included in the species *Homo erectus*

Primate: any member of the order of mammals that includes human beings as well as monkeys, apes, lorises, lemurs, bushbabies, and tarsiers

Ramapithecus: a genus of hominids living between about 16 million and 8 million years ago, found in Africa, Asia, and Europe. It is thought by some anthropologists to represent the first members of the human line.

Relative dating: determining the age of fossils or rock deposits with regard to other, similar fossils or deposits for which dates are known

Savanna: a tropical or sub-tropical grassland characterized by scattered trees or shrubs and a pronounced dry season

Sexual dimorphism: the distinct difference in form and size of the body, teeth or other structural detail between males and females of the same species

Sivapithecus: a genus of ape, found in Europe and Asia, that lived between 16 million and 8 million years ago. It is related to *Ramapithecus*.

Species: a group of living animals that can breed together and produce fertile offspring, but do not breed with members of another species; also a group of extinct animals that are characterized by the same degree of similarity that is found in a living species

Tundra: the treeless landscape of Arctic regions characterized by permanently frozen subsoil and low-growing vegetation such as mosses, lichens, herbs and shrubs

Index

Credits

The publishers gratefully acknowledge permission to reproduce the following illustrations: L. Freedman and M. Lofgren, Journal of Human Biology 8.2, © Academic Press Inc. (London) Ltd. 84; Adespoton Film Services 20, 27, 29, 33, 38, 63*t*, 67*t*, *b*, 68; L. Aiello 16; Bryan and Cherry Alexander 89*t*; American Museum of Natural History 15*bl*; P. Andrews 26 31*tl*; Ardea 9*t4*, *cl*, *c3*, *c4*, 25*b*; Bettman Archive 13*b*; J. Launois/Black Star 53*b*; Trustees of the British Museum (Natural History) 70; B. Campbell 40; Bruce Coleman 3, 9*t2*, *t3*, *br*, 41, 44, 62; Colorifc! 85*t*, 91*r*; Cooper Bridgeman Library 10; M. H. Day 32*c*, *r*, 72, 83*t*; Mary Evans 12*r*; Explorer 47; L. G. Freeman 65; Robert Harding Associates 25*t*, 63*b*; B. Barbey, Magnum/John Hillelsen Agency 53*t*; Michael Holford/Trustees of the British Museum 11*t*, 76; Eric Hosking 45; Alan Hutchison 89*br*; Illustrated London News 71; Inst. of Vertebrate Palaeontology & Palaeoanthropology, Peking 73*t*, 82; G. Isaac 48, 49; Jacana 9*tl*, *bl*, 52; G. Kennedy 86*l*; B. Ray/Life © Time Inc 1970 46; J. H. Matternes, courtesy National Geographic Society 18, 19; G. Mazza 9*c2*; M.I.S.S. Ltd. 12*l*; Musée de l'Homme 77*tr*; © National Geographic Society: D. Brill 35, M. H. Day 32*l*, H. van Lawick 36, 37; National Museums of Kenya 31*tr*, *b*; Natural History Museum of Los Angeles County 15*tl*, 86*r*; Nature Photographers 15*br*; Oxford Scientific Films/Animals Animals 9*bc*; Ann and Bury Peerless 11*b*; Pic Photos 79; Picturepoint 28; D. Pilbeam 28; J. Reader 17, 21, 34, 39, 42, 43*r*, 56*tl*, *tr*, 57, 75; Rijksmuseum van Natuurlijke Historie, Leiden 13*t*; R. Soleki 93; C. Stringer 59*b*, 66, 73*c*, *b*; A. Thorne 59*t*, 85*b*; Trewin Copplestone Books 30; Trewin Copplestone Books/Zoological Society of London 15*tr*; J. Launois/Transworld 89*bl*; B. Vandermeersch 77*tl*, 83*b*; J. Vertut 77*b*, 80; Vision International 69, 88, 90; B. A. Wood 43*l*, 56*b*; ZEFA 91*l*.

Front cover photograph: David Pilbeam

Artwork by: John Yates 17 adapted from *The Making of Mankind* by Richard E. Leakey © Sherman B.V., 6, 7, 18, 19, 22, 23, 26, 28, 39, 43, 46, 48, 50, 51, 55, 56, 59, 65, 66, 73, 77, 82, 83, 84; Bruno Elletori 45, 58, 62, 78, 79; Colin Wilson 35, 41, 64, 75; all maps Eugene Fleury except Carol McCleeve 24.

Bibliography

The Emergence of Man (3rd edn), John E. Pfeiffer, Harper and Row, 1978
The Evolution of Primate Behavior, Alison Jolly, Collier Macmillan, 1972
The Fossil Evidence: The Human Evolutionary Journey (3rd edn), F. E. Poirier, C. V. Mosby, 1981
The Fossil Evidence of Human Evolution, W. E. Le Gros Clark, University of Chicago Press, 1978
Guide to Fossil Man (3rd edn), Michael H. Day, University of Chicago Press, 1978
Lucy, Donald C. Johanson and A. Edey Maitland, Simon and Schuster, 1981
Missing Links, John Reader, Little, Brown, 1981
Origins, Richard Leakey and Roger Lewin, E. P. Dutton, 1977